Y0-BDV-071

Arthur M. Cohen
EDITOR-IN-CHIEF

Florence B. Brawer
ASSOCIATE EDITOR

Community Colleges and Proprietary Schools: Conflict or Convergence?

Darrel A. Clowes
Virginia Polytechnic Institute and State University

Elizabeth M. Hawthorne
Pennsylvania State University

EDITORS

Number 91, Fall 1995

JOSSEY-BASS PUBLISHERS
San Francisco

ERIC®

Clearinghouse for Community Colleges

COMMUNITY COLLEGES AND PROPRIETARY SCHOOLS: CONFLICT OR
CONVERGENCE?
Darrel A. Clowes, Elizabeth M. Hawthorne (eds.)
New Directions for Community Colleges, no. 91
Volume XXIII, number 3
Arthur M. Cohen, Editor-in-Chief
Florence B. Brawer, Associate Editor

Microfilm copies of issues and articles are available in 16mm and 35mm,
as well as microfiche in 105mm, through University Microfilms Inc.,
300 North Zeeb Road, Ann Arbor, Michigan 48106-1346.

LC 85-644753   ISSN 0194-3081   ISBN 0-7879-9936-9

NEW DIRECTIONS FOR COMMUNITY COLLEGES is part of The Jossey-Bass
Higher and Adult Education Series and is published quarterly by Jossey-
Bass Inc., Publishers, 350 Sansome Street, San Francisco, California
94104-1342 in association with the ERIC Clearinghouse for Community
Colleges. Second-class postage paid at San Francisco, California, and at
additional mailing offices. POSTMASTER: Send address changes to New
Directions for Community Colleges, Jossey-Bass Inc., Publishers, 350
Sansome Street, San Francisco, California 94104-1342.

SUBSCRIPTIONS for 1995 cost $49.00 for individuals and $72.00 for institutions, agencies, and libraries.

THE MATERIAL in this publication is based on work sponsored wholly or
in part by the Office of Educational Research and Improvement, U.S.
Department of Education, under contract number RI-93-00-2003. Its con-
tents do not necessarily reflect the views of the Department, or any other
agency of the U.S. Government.

EDITORIAL CORRESPONDENCE should be sent to the Editor-in-Chief, Arthur
M. Cohen, at the ERIC Clearinghouse for Community Colleges, Univer-
sity of California, 3051 Moore Hall, Mailbox 951521, 405 Hilgard Avenue,
Los Angeles, California 90024-1521.

Cover photograph © Rene Sheret, After Image, Los Angeles, California,
1990.

TCF Manufactured in the United States of America on Lyons Falls
Pathfinder Tradebook. This paper is acid-free and 100 percent
totally chlorine-free.

CONTENTS

EDITORS' NOTES

Readers will note that this volume is organized around topics that both describe the proprietary school and explore the areas of convergence with and divergence from the community college. The development of this volume begins with Darrel Clowes's chapter. He depicts higher education using a feudal-age metaphor. Proprietary schools are the hunters and gatherers far outside the castle keep, and the community colleges are located outside the castle walls in the villages around the castle. He artfully puts forth the hypothesis that community colleges and career colleges are becoming more and more alike as the hunters and gatherers make incursions into the villages and adopt many of their customs. At the same time, the villagers ape some of the practices of the hunters and gatherers. Each of the remaining authors was invited to respond to this thesis in the context of their individual topics.

This volume was written for community college educators—faculty and administrators—and trustees to inform them about the proprietary sector of postsecondary education in the United States. Why this audience? Why this topic? Why now?

Our experience with community colleges and proprietary schools has taught us that there is little cooperation or communication between individual institutions, nor are there any formal or informal linkages at the state or national levels. Still, there are points of contact with respect to organization, accreditation, curriculum, and students. We note here that little is known systematically about faculty or pedagogy in proprietary schools, and we can only hope that this volume will prompt serious inquiry in these areas. We offer an introduction to proprietary schools or, as they have most recently been named, "career colleges," in the context of postsecondary education in the United States. We assume that readers have a basic understanding of community colleges and are curious about career colleges.

In Chapter Two, Jon Hittman initiates newcomers into the world of proprietary schools in the conclusion of the twentieth century. He delineates points of intersection and separation of community colleges and proprietary schools with respect to the organization and administration of these schools and colleges. He notes points of convergence that he argues should be explored and developed.

Craig Honick, in Chapter Three, addresses historical perspectives on proprietary schools in the United States. This history is an important contribution toward breaking new ground in our understanding of the proprietary sector. Honick introduces the reader to the forces that fostered the development of these schools. That the proprietary sector has a long tradition in the United States is important in informing our understanding of its place in the scheme of postsecondary education.

An analysis of the relationship of the curricula provided by career colleges and community colleges is presented in Chapter Four by Cheryl Hyslop and Michael Parsons. Their presentation highlights the need for both kinds of institutions to have in place a process of curriculum development and review that can enable them to adapt to rapid change in the environment. They cite models of collaboration and communication that similar institutions might adapt to suit local needs. Indeed, if there is convergence, there are opportunities for cooperation that will allow community colleges and career colleges to work together more effectively.

Xing David Cheng and Bernard Levin offer an analysis of the students enrolled in career colleges in Chapter Five. They show that there is a fascinating range of students that are often not served by community colleges. Further, they highlight some differences between for-profit career colleges and the small number of not-for-profit career colleges, an important distinction not made in the literature thus far.

Carolyn Prager, in Chapter Six, deftly explores the pertinent issues of accreditation and the unique aspects of career colleges that have become degree-granting institutions. She makes manifest areas where communication between the two kinds of institutions is essential. Her examination of how accreditation has played a major role in shaping career colleges is instructive. Because the world of accreditation is changing rapidly, dramatically, and forcefully, additional modifications to accreditation may well have been made since this chapter was written.

Chapter Seven, by Richard Moore, focuses on the policy interests of the federal government with respect to career colleges and the implications for practitioners in both career colleges and community colleges. Moore disagrees with Clowes's argument that there is growing convergence and brings to this volume yet another spirited discussion asking whether this apparent convergence is forced or organic.

Chapter Eight, by Bruce Chaloux, examines the role of the states in monitoring and evaluating the career colleges. Here, Chaloux shows how the relationships among the traditional oversight triad of American higher education—the federal government, the state governments, and the accrediting associations—is changing, in large measure (but not exclusively) due to the introduction of proprietary schools into the provinces of traditional higher education. He explores the implications for higher education and raises the issue of how technology in higher education may alter the relationships even further. Chaloux presents proprietary sector views of the changing oversight scene that are instructive for readers from traditional higher education.

The final chapter, by Elizabeth Hawthorne, draws conclusions about the thesis of convergence between the proprietary and community college sectors of postsecondary education.

We cannot, however, present a complete picture of career colleges, because there has been limited scholarly interest in them and therefore limited data about them. We do, however, offer a broad view of career colleges and an extensive combined bibliography of research and comment on them. Hence, we hope to accomplish the second purpose of this volume, which is to stimulate scholarly inquiry about them.

The implications of the expanding sector of postsecondary education are significant for policy makers at the federal, state, and institutional levels. Limited resources necessitate a more comprehensive examination of education for work—the essence of the career college—that will yield a more effective and efficient use of resources. We welcome your responses to this work.

Darrel A. Clowes
Elizabeth M. Hawthorne
Editors

DARREL A. CLOWES is associate professor in the College of Education at Virginia Polytechnic Institute and State University in Blacksburg.

ELIZABETH M. HAWTHORNE is associate professor and director of academic affairs at Pennsylvania State University, Berks Campus, Reading.

The thesis of convergence of community colleges and proprietary schools is put forward; reactions are solicited from the authors that follow and from readers.

Community Colleges and Proprietary Schools: Conflict or Convergence?

Darrel A. Clowes

Proprietary schools are silent partners in American higher education. The *Encyclopedia of Higher Education* (Clark and Neave, 1992) illustrates the recognition accorded the proprietary school by the rest of higher education: out of almost 300 entries, the *Encyclopedia* gives proprietary higher education one entry. None of the ninety-seven topical chapters in the nine published volumes of the *Higher Education Handbook of Theory and Research* (Smart, 1985–1993) is devoted to, or even addresses, this topic. The ASHE-ERIC Higher Education Reports series has issued eighty-two reports from its inception in 1984 to 1993; only one report was devoted to proprietary schools. The periodical literature in higher education is similarly sparse on this topic, yet there were approximately 4,000 accredited proprietary institutions enrolling an estimated 1,800,000 students in 1987 (in addition to another 1,500,000 students enrolled in home-study courses) (Lee and Merisotis, 1991). The 1989–90 National Postsecondary Student Aid Survey data show that proprietary schools enrolled 6.1 percent of all postsecondary education students, and these students received 23.1 percent of the Pell grants and 31.9 percent of the federally guaranteed student loans (Grubb, 1993). They also are estimated to have provided more than 50 percent of the student loan defaults (Fraas, 1990, p. 40). This high default rate and the growing awareness of the significant involvement of proprietary school students in federal and state financial aid programs has attracted recent interest and publicity.

As proprietary schools move into the limelight as an element in the public policy discussion over student loan programs, the limited information about the institutions and their relationship to other sectors of postsecondary education becomes important. Federal, regional, and state policy makers have a distressing history of treating all institutions of higher education as if they were alike, despite the Carnegie classification scheme (Carnegie Foundation for the Advancement of Teaching, 1994) and despite substantial research to support differences. Research universities have different purposes and clientele than regional colleges, and both differ from community colleges; yet policy makers routinely aggregate the institutions under the same financial aid regulations and accountability measures.

A significant issue arises when a publicly sponsored institution like the community college is considered to be of the same type as a private institution like the proprietary school. This highlights the issue of whether differences in purpose, form, and substance warrant differential treatments. Within postsecondary education, the community college and the proprietary or career school are most alike. That relationship is the "hot spot" where proprietary institutions and postsecondary education intersect. This volume addresses that relationship in order to inform policy makers of the underlying issues involved in treating the institutions as though they were alike. Equally important is the need for leaders in the institutions to realize the dangers of decisions that serve short-term ends—decisions to increase or restrict enrollment growth and economize on operation—but that carry long-term consequences. The institutions thus lose their distinctive features and begin to converge with another institutional type. The result could be positive, but it is more likely that institutions will lose their purpose and identity and society will lose a desired service. On a variety of indicators, this convergence appears to be happening to the community college and the private proprietary school sectors.

How does traditional higher education, and especially the community college, relate to proprietary schools? The first question is, How would anyone know? Higher education is a diverse and confusing enterprise and a rather ill-defined activity. To approach the question, it is helpful to examine the key terms: *higher education, postsecondary education, community college,* and *proprietary school.* Each term is used as if its meaning were clear and as if the term represented a fixed phenomenon in our society. However, one can argue that each term is actually a label for changing phenomena and that understanding the changing phenomena is essential for understanding how higher education generally, and the community college specifically, relate to the proprietary school.

Language Shifts and a Sea Change

We live in a dynamic society, and one of the keys to understanding the changes in society is to understand the changes in the language we use to represent phenomena. Language shifts are indicators of societal change in the same way that mist and white caps are the indicators of a sea change. Four terms are central to this argument for a societal change. The first is *higher education.* That is no longer a very descriptive term. For example, about fifteen years ago the American Educational Research Association set up a new division—Division J—to represent the traditional field of higher education. In meetings and discussions about what to call this new division, members acknowledged that the division was to include not only graduate and professional schools and four-year colleges and universities but also community colleges, trade schools, and many adult training activities. Many felt they could not call those latter endeavors higher education, so a compromise term was decided upon—*postsecondary education*. And that term is used in the division today. That decision and the earlier use of the term in the 1972 amendments to the Higher Education Act of 1954 represented a sea change in higher education as a field. The field now includes other types of institutions and does other kinds of things than those traditionally associated with the Stanfords and Yales of this world.

The American community college has been evolving over the past century. Numerous writers have attempted to capture the direction of that evolution and to predict or recommend future directions. (See, for example, McCartan, 1983; Deegan and Tillery, 1985; and Teitel, 1991.) A strong movement toward an increasingly vocational orientation has been identified and documented (Brint and Karabel, 1989; Clowes and Levin, 1989; Harris and Grede, 1977). A parallel long-term decline in the transfer function of community colleges has been well documented (Grubb, 1991; Lombardi, 1979; Pincus and Archer, 1989). Teitel (1991) has proposed that the traditional pattern of vertical integration within the educational system with transfer from secondary schools to community colleges to four-year institutions or to work has been superseded by a pattern of horizontal integration. This horizontal integration links the community college with business, government, and industry through customized training and other client-specific training and educational activities delivered on campus, on site, and on client demand. This linkage is provided by the continuing education arm of the community college and challenges the mainstream curriculum arm of the college as the dominant function of the institution.

An interesting implication of Teitel's proposition is that horizontal integration through continuing education activities represents an opportunity for the institution to generate funding other than the monies provided by public support. The curricular programs and the vertical integration they represent remain tied to public funding and, in most states, cannot generate so-called discretionary monies or risk capital as the horizontally integrated programs can. Since community colleges are public agencies with public oversight of appropriated funds, the opportunity to raise discretionary monies free of public oversight is very attractive. These training activities have been described as the "cash cow" of postsecondary education ("Cash Cow", May 15, 1991). Whether the community college has a strong transfer orientation and vertical linkage, a strong vocational orientation and horizontal linkage, or is taking on a remedial orientation as argued by McGrath and Spear (1991), it is clear that the institution is evolving in its primary functions and its relations to other aspects of postsecondary education.

A series of language shifts involving the association representing the two-year institutions illustrates this nicely. The association, begun as the American Association of Junior Colleges in the 1920s, became the American Association of Community and Junior Colleges in the 1950s, and flirted with becoming the American Association of Community, Junior, and Technical Colleges in the 1980s. In the 1990s, it has become the American Association of Community Colleges—another element of the sea change.

Proprietary institutions in the United States have also been evolving. From modest colonial origins, the institutions have emerged as key players in the preparation of the U.S. workforce. Growth was spurred by the G.I. Bill after World War II and again by the student aid policies of the 1970s and 1980s. Today, these institutions are significant providers of training under the Job Training Partnership Act (JTPA), of entry-level skill training beyond the secondary schools, and of occupationally oriented education at the certificate, associate, and even the bachelor's degree levels (Bender, 1991). Some institutions are accredited by the traditional regional accrediting associations serving higher education; more are accredited by national and state voluntary accrediting associations for proprietary institutions; and almost all are accredited by state licensing agencies.

Another language shift is occurring. When insiders talk about proprietary schools, they use the term *career colleges*. The accrediting association for these institutions is now the Accrediting Commission of Career Schools and Colleges of Technology, and their professional association is the Career College Association. This language shift, like that involving the American Association of Community Colleges, represents how the involved institutions would like to be perceived. This is a different form of language shift than that originating from the society at large, but it is still a language shift. This shift represents another element in the sea change occurring in our postsecondary institutions.

A Metaphor

If the basic terms in this analysis—higher education, postsecondary education, community college, and proprietary school—are involved in language shifts and represent aspects of a dynamic situation, how can the relationships among them be assessed and presented? Metaphor can create meaning by relating known elements to the unknown. A metaphor is inexact but occasionally elegant; it often provides insight into a context and into the relationships among the parts. The architecture of the medieval period serves as a metaphor to illustrate this situation.

Medieval castles were built to represent and to defend the body politic. The castle as metaphor is centered on the castle keep—the location within the stronghold and its fortified walls—where the core of the body politic is protected. It is where they put the princess and where the king and the queen retreat when all else is lost. Around the castle keep is a fortified inner city, a defensive area surrounded by a high interior wall. Outside this inner high wall is the outer section of the city, then a final wall, and then ultimately the moat. Outside the moat are the fields upon which the city and its castle depend for food and the fortified hamlets where the farm workers live. Beyond the fields and hamlets lies the wilderness. How does the castle and its fortified city relate to higher education? Imagine higher education as a differentiated and hierarchical system. The elite institutions forming the core of higher education are the castle keep—the area of most sanctity and importance, the area all else must protect. These are the research universities and the selective liberal arts colleges. Then, outside the castle keep but within the high interior wall is the inner city; the regional universities made up of doctoral colleges and universities reside here. Between the inner wall and the outer castle wall and its moat are the dwellings of the city's traders and craftspeople—the comprehensive colleges and universities and the nonselective liberal arts colleges. Outside the moat and beyond the drawbridge are the fortified villages—the community colleges.

When the Visigoths appear on the horizon, the dynamics of the metaphor come into play. The first line of defense is outside the walls in the fortified villages. The main body of the army withdraws behind the walls, and the drawbridges are raised. Indeed, they snap shut. The Visigoths attack the fortified villages and rape and pillage in the fields. The hope is that the Visigoths will accept the easy pickings and move on, leaving the city within the walls, the castle, and especially the castle keep unviolated. In this scenario, the fortified villages, as the first line of defense, represent the function the community college serves for higher education when new client groups, new societal demands, or severe financial stresses are imposed on higher education. The metaphor says that a primary function of the community colleges is to protect the castle keep—to protect higher education and its traditional functions. The metaphor also implies that community colleges are not really full partners in higher education. In bad times, one can almost hear the drawbridge snapping shut.

Where are proprietary schools in this metaphor? They are the trappers in the hills beyond the fields; they are out there hunting and gathering and trying to stay alive, too. They are the first given up, then the community colleges, and so on. The metaphor suggests that traditional higher education, which has to do with the castle keep, is part, but only a small part, of postsecondary education.

In summary, postsecondary education today has much in common with the medieval fortified city and its environs. The established institutions and their social and intellectual functions represent the most valued aspects of higher education. They are protected from all threats. The newer institutions providing less-valued services and serving less-valued clients are protected, but not at all costs. These newer institutions of postsecondary education, their functions, and their clients are outside the walls of tradition, wealth, and perceived quality. They are beyond the moat and on the penumbra—the blurred edge—of postsecondary education.

Institutions Compared

Community colleges and career colleges are both institutions on the penumbra of postsecondary education. How are community colleges and career colleges becoming alike? Let me count the ways, first from the perspective of the community college and then from the perspective of the career college. Community colleges are commonly portrayed as degree-granting and transfer-oriented institutions, while career colleges are not. However, any scholar of community colleges knows that is no longer true. A very modest proportion of the enrollees receive or even aspire to the associate degree, and the rate of transfer is also extremely modest (Cohen and Brawer, 1982; Dougherty, 1992; Grubb, 1991; Pascarella and Terenzini, 1991). There is little difference on those criteria between community colleges and career schools. Neither confers associate degrees on, or is a vehicle for transfer for, a significant minority of its enrollees (Cheng, Clowes, and Muffo, 1992).

A second proposed difference is that community colleges offer general education as a strong component of their curriculum, while career colleges do not. This links the community college with higher education as it is traditionally defined and distinguishes it from the proprietary sector. However, the work of Cohen (1987) and Eaton (1988) suggests that those general education functions have gradually eroded within the community college. Cohen and Brawer (1987) document the preponderance of service, remedial, and introductory courses in the community college curriculum and the paucity of sequential and integrative courses necessary for a strong general education curriculum. Career colleges, on the other hand, are increasingly forced by accreditation standards to offer degree programs with general education requirements comparable to those of the community college. So, that difference disappears. At the program level, the institutions are coming to resemble each other.

A third presumed difference is the collegiate culture and academic orientation of the community college, as contrasted with the nonacademic and training orientation of the career college. Studies of community college culture challenge this difference. London (1978), Richardson, Fisk, and Okun (1983), and Weis (1985) document a culture within community colleges oppositional to the academic culture associated with higher education. McGrath and Spear (1991) extend this analysis to portray the culture of the open-access community college as a culture distinctly different from that of traditional higher education. This culture is a unique blend of characteristics of the open-access comprehensive high school, the academic culture of higher education, the remedial programs that permeate the curriculum, and the vocational emphasis of many of the institutions. Career colleges share many of these characteristics, including the increasing influence of the academic culture. Thus, another area of difference is dwindling.

A fourth area of perceived difference is that community colleges are publicly funded while career colleges are not. However, public funds flow into proprietary schools under the guise of student financial aid. These institutions are basically publicly funded, but different vehicles are used to get the money to them (Fraas, 1990). So, that distinction also fades.

A final area of difference that would appear to hold is the public control and the not-for-profit orientation of the community college compared to the private control and for-profit orientation typical of the proprietary institution.

Here, differences do exist, but the differences are not as clear as they appear on the surface. Community colleges are regulated by state and professional accreditation agencies as well as local and state governing boards. Proprietary institutions are increasingly regulated by state and professional accreditation agencies, since accreditation is necessary if students are to be eligible for state or federal financial aid. Accreditation demands bring the two types of institutions closer and closer together in curriculum, financial aid policies, and management practices. Proprietary institutions are open about their for-profit orientation. Community colleges are increasingly constrained by limited state and local financial support. A frequent recourse is using continuing education offerings and contract training to generate extra money and risk capital ("Cash Cow," 1991). This discretionary money is not profit, but it is used, as profit would be, for program support and expansion if not for salaries and bonuses.

Do differences emerge if we approach from the perspective of proprietary schools and career colleges themselves? Career college curricula are organized around utilitarian and short-term programs. Is that a distinction? Research using a national sample of the transcripts of community college students concludes that most community college students use the institution for five to six courses in a ten-year period and that the majority of the courses taken are vocational in nature (Adelman, 1992). It appears that the community college curriculum is a short-term and utilitarian curriculum also. Difference based upon curriculum use does not hold.

Another possible difference is that career colleges are outside the system of graded education. But, community colleges, with their weak transfer function and their few degree recipients, also have a weak claim to a place within the system of graded education. Further, as the community college becomes more vocationally oriented, increasingly provides contract training programs for business and industry, and offers significantly greater portions of its instruction off campus through continuing education and adult education programs, it moves further outside the system of graded education. Many community colleges have emphasized horizontal linkages to their community and their local business and industry at the expense of the vertical linkages within graded education represented by transfer connections with local high schools, colleges, and universities (Clowes and Levin, 1989; Teitel, 1991). Again, the distinction does not hold. One of the criticisms of proprietary schools over the years has been that they contribute to social reproduction and stratification, although little evidence can be produced to substantiate the criticism (Lee and Merisotis, 1990). Yet, the critics of the community college say that is exactly what the community colleges began to do back in the 1960s and 1970s (Karabel, 1972; Zwerling, 1976) and continue to do today (Dougherty, 1991). So, that distinction breaks down.

For career colleges, convergence is seen in the increased attention to accreditation and accreditation standards and to becoming degree-granting. The accountability movement is now affecting career colleges through federal legislation related to accountability for student aid and to monitoring student progress. This is similar to the accountability requirements emerging for community colleges and is another move toward convergence. Finally, the emerging pattern of career colleges moving from primarily certificate-granting institutions to institutions that also offer the associate degree represents convergence.

In many ways, community colleges and career colleges are converging. However, some distinctions do seem real. At a superficial level, community colleges are generally larger and have a more comprehensive curriculum; career colleges are smaller and have a more specialized curriculum. A more significant distinction lies in the students served. Community colleges primarily serve the third of the population classified as middle-class. The career colleges primarily serve the next lower third of the population labeled the working-class (Gilbert and Kahl, 1982, pp. 343–356).

Another difference lies in the characteristics of the two student bodies. Community college students are primarily white, primarily female, and have moderate aspirations for further education and for careers. In career colleges, more students are from a minority group; the proportion of females is higher than in the community colleges; and the students have lower aspirations (Cheng, Clowes, and Muffo, 1992; Grubb, 1991). Another difference may exist in the market they target. The community college increasingly prepares people for what they will do after initial job entry. Retraining, training on the job, and training for a career change are becoming the hallmarks of community colleges. Career colleges focus on preparing their students with entry-level occupational skills. Both institutional types serve a significant social purpose: they provide an avenue for upward mobility in our work-based society. However, one institutional type has service to its students and its community as a primary goal; the other has profit for its owners as a primary goal.

Differences between the institution types remain, but the differences are modest and diminishing. The histories of the two institutional types show different origins and different orientations, but the informal system of higher education in the United States is dynamic and permeable. Social and economic forces have operated to cause changes in the roles of institutions within the system and in the roles of the system itself. Proprietary institutions and corporate colleges have converted to not-for-profit, baccalaureate-granting institutions; community colleges have become four-year institutions; and single-purpose institutions have become comprehensive (Nash and Hawthorne, 1987). Concurrently, the system has operated to protect itself and its core functions from change. Thus, two institutional types on the penumbra of higher education—the career college and the community college—have been driven toward apparent convergence. They now exist outside the moat; they exist on the margin. That may be the essential thing they have in common, because each has a tenuous relationship with higher education while maintaining a strong role in postsecondary education.

If mission defines an institution, these two types should look very different because one has service to students and community as its mission, and the other has profit as a mission. Yet, they appear to be converging in form and perhaps in substance. Of concern is how they relate to each other and how they each relate to the balance of the institutions in postsecondary education. Should public policy treat them and other institutional types in postsecondary education the same? Will that treatment drive them more toward convergence? Is that a good thing for society? Can social purpose coexist with a profit motive in an educational setting? These questions are the focus of our exploration.

If the community college is indeed outside the moat, it needs to be concerned about the role of the proprietary school or career college, because the two institutional sectors are becoming more alike than different. The shifts described here illustrate that convergence.

Conclusion

I have argued that community colleges and career colleges are each undergoing a sea change, indeed, that all of postsecondary education has been undergoing a sea change. Higher education, using the metaphor of the castle, has acted to protect itself and the revered functions of the elite institutions by spawning a host of lesser or different institutions to absorb the buffeting presented by society. Society has pressured higher education to advance social justice through increased access, to enhance community and economic development through applied research and technical training, and to maintain standards with reduced resources. Society also desires to protect the knowledge-producing activities of higher education for their economic, scientific, and social contributions. Hence, the postsecondary institutions have come under stress and have responded. A significant aspect of that response has been for some institutions to lose their distinctive characteristics and purposes.

Public policy that ignores differences among institutional types and treats all in the same way has been a contributor to this process. Current public policies on student financial aid and on institutional accountability are examples of this activity and contribute to its negative consequences.

I argue in this chapter that career colleges and community colleges are becoming increasingly alike in providing a specialized form of education and training beyond secondary school. They are emerging as institutions with different histories but perhaps a shared future. Certainly, they have an uneasy present, as each type needs to sort out and identify its priorities, roles, and future to allow for wise planning. The situation is confounded by the reality that each institution is unique and few community colleges or career colleges can be easily categorized. Indeed, there is often as much difference within an institutional type as there is between institutional types. Yet, it is important to differentiate among institutional types for the benefit of those involved with public policy and for those responsible for institutional leadership. This chapter and this volume are designed to inform and to stimulate that discussion.

References

Adelman, C. *The Way We Are: The Community College as American Thermometer.* Washington, D.C.: U.S. Department of Education, 1992.

Bender, L. W. "Applied Associate Degree Transfer Phenomenon: Proprietaries and Publics." *Community College Review,* 1991, *19* (3), 22–29.

Brint, S., and Karabel, J. *The Diverted Dream: Community Colleges and the Promise of Educational Opportunity in America, 1900–1985.* New York: Oxford University Press, 1989.

Carnegie Foundation for the Advancement of Teaching. *Carnegie Classification of Institutions of Higher Education. A Technical Report.* Princeton, N.J.: Princeton University Press, 1994.

"Cash Cow." *Chronicle of Higher Education,* May 15, 1991, p. 1.

Cheng, X., Clowes, D. A., and Muffo, J. A. "Assessing the Educational Attainment of Proprietary School Students from National Data." Unpublished report, 1992. (ED 342 458)

Clark, B., and Neave, G. (eds.). *Encyclopedia of Higher Education.* Elmsford, N.Y.: Pergamon Press, 1992.

Clowes, D. A., and Levin, B. H. "Community, Technical, and Junior Colleges: Are They Leaving Higher Education?" *Journal of Higher Education,* 1989, *60,* 350–355.

Cohen, A. M., and Brawer, F. B. *The American Community College.* San Francisco: Jossey-Bass, 1982.

Cohen, A. M., and Brawer, F. B. *The Collegiate Function of Community Colleges: Fostering Higher Learning Through Curriculum and Student Transfer.* San Francisco: Jossey-Bass, 1987.

Deegan, W. L., Tillery, D., and Associates. *Renewing the American Community College: Priorities and Strategies for Effective Leadership.* San Francisco: Jossey-Bass, 1985.

Dougherty, K. J. "The Community College at the Crossroads: The Need for Structural Reform." *Harvard Educational Review,* 1991, *61,* 311–336.

Dougherty, K. J. "Community Colleges and Baccalaureate Attainment." *Journal of Higher Education,* 1992, *63,* 188–214.

Eaton, J. E. *Colleges of Choice: The Enabling Impact of the Community College.* Washington, D.C.: American Council on Education, 1988.

Fraas, C. "Proprietary Schools and Student Financial Aid Programs: Background and Policy Issues." Washington, D.C.: Congressional Research Service, Library of Congress, 1990. (ED 332 623)

Gilbert, D., and Kahl, J. A. *The American Class Structure: A New Synthesis.* Homewood, Ill.: Dorsey Press, 1982.

Grubb, W. N. "The Decline of Community College Transfer Rates: Evidence from National Longitudinal Surveys." *Journal of Higher Education,* 1991, *62,* 194–223.

Grubb, W. N. "The Long-Run Effects of Proprietary Schools on Wages and Earnings: Implications for Federal Policy." *Educational Evaluation and Policy Analysis,* 1993, *15,* 17–33.

Harris, N. C., and Grede, J. F. *Career Education in Colleges: A Guide for Planning Two- and Four-Year Occupational Programs.* San Francisco: Jossey-Bass, 1977.

Karabel, J. "Community Colleges and Social Stratification." *Harvard Educational Review,* 1972, *42,* 521–562.

Lee, J. B., and Merisotis, J. P. *Proprietary Schools: Programs, Policies, and Prospects.* ASHE-ERIC Higher Education Report No. 5. Washington, D.C.: Association for the Study of Higher Education, 1990. (ED 331 337)

Lee, J. B., and Merisotis, J. "Private Career Schools: An Objective Look." *Career Training,* Mar. 1991, pp. 28–31.

Lombardi, J. "The Decline of Transfer Education." Paper No. 70. Los Angeles: ERIC Clearinghouse for Junior Colleges, 1979. (ED 179 273)

London, H. B. *Culture of a Community College.* New York: Praeger, 1978.

McCartan, A. M. "The Community College Mission: Present Challenges and Future Visions." *Harvard Educational Review,* 1983, *54,* 676–690.

McGrath, D., and Spear, M. B. *The Academic Crisis of the Community College.* Albany: State University of New York Press, 1991.

Nash, N. S., and Hawthorne, E. M. *The Formal Recognition of Corporate Education: Conflict and Collegiality in Postsecondary Education.* ASHE-ERIC Higher Education Report No. 3. Washington, D.C.: Association for the Study of Higher Education, 1987. (ED 286 437)

Pascarella, E. T., and Terenzini, P. J. *How College Affects Students: Findings and Insights from Twenty Years of Research.* San Francisco: Jossey-Bass, 1991.

Pincus, F., and Archer, E. *Bridges to Opportunity: Are Community Colleges Meeting the Transfer Needs of Minority Students?* New York: Academy for Educational Development and College Entrance Examination Board, 1989.

Richardson, R. C., Jr., Fisk, E. C., and Okun, M. A. *Literacy in the Open-Access College.* San Francisco: Jossey-Bass, 1983.

Smart, J. C. (ed.). *Higher Education Handbook of Theory and Research.* Vols. 1–10. New York: Agathon Press, 1985–1993.

Teitel, L. "The Transformation of a Community College." *Community College Review,* 1991, *19* (1), 7–13.

Weis, L. *Between Two Worlds: Black Students in an Urban Community College.* New York: Routledge & Kegan Paul, 1985.

Zwerling, L. S. *Second Best: The Crisis of the Community College.* New York: McGraw-Hill, 1976.

DARREL A. CLOWES is associate professor in the College of Education at Virginia Polytechnic Institute and State University in Blacksburg.

The author describes the forces operating on proprietary schools and their transition into career colleges. The ways in which these institutions are becoming more like community colleges are also discussed.

Changes in Mission, Governance, and Funding of Proprietary Postsecondary Institutions

Jon A. Hittman

Private, for-profit postsecondary educational institutions are trade, technical, business, cosmetology, and barber schools that are privately owned and managed and are both service-oriented and profit-motivated, according to Fulton (1969). Proprietary schools have been important but unheralded contributors to the American system of postsecondary education and training. They are driven by the profit motive, which has been spurned by the traditional academic community. Also, they have not been perceived as competing with the traditional delivery system of public postsecondary, or higher education (Erwin, 1975). Debate during the 1992 reauthorization of the Higher Education Act (HEA) has altered the prevailing impression of dissimilarity of mission and has catapulted career colleges into the consciousness of public policy makers and public postsecondary education leaders alike.

The revelation of rising default rates on student loans, statistics regarding program completion and placement rates, and accusations of consumer abuse have triggered heated debate about the quality and effectiveness of education delivered at all postsecondary institutions. During this debate, all postsecondary institutions have attempted to explain their outcomes in terms of functions, operations, and student characteristics in an effort to justify continued access to publicly subsidized funding. In addition, they also have expressed their concerns to policy makers regarding regulatory constraints that are perceived to be onerous. In the aftermath of this prolonged and frequently intense debate, there is a growing perception that a similarity of circumstance exists between community colleges and proprietary institutions. This chapter supports the convergence theme of the monograph by providing a description of the traditional and changing mission, internal governance, and funding of proprietary postsecondary institutions and comparing career colleges and community colleges in relation to these topics.

Traditional Proprietary School Mission

Factors that created a market niche for providers of vocational training include rapid industrialization, a student and employer market base that had not been traditionally courted or served adequately by public institutions (Carr, 1980), and the inefficiency of the American apprenticeship system in providing business and occupational training (Tonne, 1954). Proprietary school owners responded to marketplace demands from employers for trained labor by providing short-term instruction in specific subjects with immediate employment for graduates as the prime objective (Shoemaker, 1973).

For the purposes of this chapter, occupational or vocational training is defined as those activities designed to improve performance on a specific job that the student is currently doing or intends to do immediately upon completion of the course of study. The purpose of occupational training is to either introduce a new behavior or modify an existing behavior so that a particular and specified kind of workplace performance is achieved. Education, in contrast to occupational training, is designed to improve the student's overall competence, is transferable beyond the workplace, and is frequently more academic in nature.

The primary purpose of the traditional proprietary school was to provide vocational training designed to provide the graduate with entry-level work skills with which to secure immediate employment. The success of proprietary schools has been attributed to the traditional characteristics of flexibility and specialization of service (Carr, 1980). Since they depend solely on the marketplace for revenue (through tuition and fees), successful proprietary institutions have historically exhibited the following characteristics that directly support their vocational training mission:

Rapid response to provide training for new technologies as soon as they develop (Clark and Sloan, 1966)

Emphasis on programs of shorter duration focusing on hands-on training as opposed to abstract or theory-based education

Development of the placement function designed to provide employment for the graduate (Simmons, 1975)

Flexible program and course schedules designed to increase accessibility (Belitsky, 1969)

Flexible curricula designed to make it easy for the student to enter, exit, and re-enter, thereby increasing the probability of enrollment and completion (Erickson, 1972)

Flexible instruction to accommodate special student needs for individual attention, help, and encouragement (Kincaid and Podesta, 1966)

Sensitivity and responsiveness to changes in level of demand for trained man-
power and emphasis on curriculum objectives (Katz, 1973) that reflect current hiring criteria (Simmons, 1975).

Traditional proprietary schools were able to capitalize on these characteristics because those schools were more autonomous and subject to less
governmental and accrediting body oversight than traditional public postsecondary institutions.

Changing Mission

The traditional mission of the proprietary school was predicated on short-term,
focused instruction, with the objective of immediate entry-level employment.
The original mission of the community college was more comprehensive in
nature but emphasized the academic transfer function.

For proprietary schools, milestones such as access for their students to
federal programs (for example, the G.I. Bill and amendments to the HEA) were
accompanied by state approval, accreditation, and compliance with federal regulations. This has enabled proprietary schools to offer longer programs that
are taught by instructors with higher academic credentials, and has allowed
them to pursue degree-granting authority in increasing numbers. The objective of employment for graduates has not been altered, but the path to program completion has been changed and is symbolized by the change in the
name of these institutions from *trade schools* to *career colleges*.

Funding of Proprietary Institutions

Proprietary schools have traditionally depended on student-paid tuition and
fees for revenue. While this is still true, proprietary school students have
become increasingly dependent on Title IV aid, since the reauthorization of the
1972 HEA. According to a recent study, 78 percent of proprietary school students receive federal assistance of some kind (Merisotis, 1991). A U.S. Department of Education study reveals that proprietary school students account for
36.7 percent of all those who borrow and 36.4 percent of the total dollars bor-
rowed in the guaranteed student loan program during fiscal year 1989. This
federal aid is available in the form of grants and loans, and it helps eligible students finance their education. Federal financial assistance for students enrolled
in proprietary institutions began with the G.I. Bill. This highly successful bill
rewarded veterans for their service by providing federal financial support for
pursuit of postsecondary education. The educational demand created by the
veterans was for noncollegiate vocational courses. Proprietary schools were eligible to participate in the veterans program as long as they achieved federal
and state approval. The G.I. Bill set the precedent for future broad-based fed-

eral assistance for postsecondary education institutions, including proprietary schools.

Amendments to the HEA in 1972 established the Basic Educational Opportunity Grant (BEOG), which was later renamed "Pell grant" for Senator Claiborne Pell, and the Student Loan Marketing Association (Sallie Mae). These amendments were designed to give students greater access to postsecondary education. The original purpose of the BEOG, which is based on economic need, was to reduce or eliminate financial barriers for those seeking a post-secondary education. Sallie Mae provided liquidity to lenders, thereby stimulating student participation in the guaranteed student loan program. Current student financial aid programs include a maze of campus-based and federal grant, loan, and work-study programs.

Funding Summary

Arguments pointing out important differences between career colleges and community colleges can be made on the grounds that the career college is a private enterprise and the community college is a public entity. This fundamental fact is clear. However, in a global sense, both career colleges and community colleges rely on public sources for funding. In the case of the career college, the dependence is indirect because it is the student's responsibility to apply for grants and loans based on need and to repay publicly subsidized loans. Nevertheless, the majority of prospective career college students require some federal subsidy such as loans, grants, or both. In the case of the community college, the dependence is direct. Local taxes, state subsidies—by formula or proceeds from state lotteries—and funding from federal grants is received by the college directly. Student-paid tuition is a source of funding for community colleges, but the existence of these aforementioned resources allows tuition to remain low in comparison to other postsecondary institutions.

Governance

All educational institutions require some form of governance. The state and local mechanisms for governance and oversight differ from state to state and organization to organization. Traditional proprietary schools organized themselves to capitalize on the characteristics of customer responsiveness (to students and employers), practical curricula, and flexibility. Since they were private, for-profit entities, there was minimal state oversight until the proprietary school students became eligible for federal subsidies. At that point, state approval and accreditation became requirements. What is important to note is that modern career colleges are affected by federal, state, and accrediting governance.

Historically, it has been rare for private, for-profit institutions to have a board of lay trustees to which the campus-level chief administrator reports. Pursuit of degree-granting status requires the establishment of a board of trustees made up of individuals who represent the institution's constituency—faculty, students, and supporters. The composition of this board diffuses the decision-making authority for control of the institution, which consequently adversely affects the speed and flexibility with which the institution can respond to the fluid postsecondary education environment.

Administration. In order for proprietary institutions to function effectively, they developed a structure to execute the necessary core functions of organizational leadership, financial administration, recruitment of students, delivery of education and training, and student services emphasizing graduate placement. The most common organizational structure consists of the administration and four divisions or departments: recruitment and admissions; finance and financial aid; education; and student services, retention, and placement services.

The campus-level chief administrator may have one of several different titles such as president, executive director, or director. The person holding this position is responsible for campus-level leadership and the overall operation of the institution. The administration is responsible for creating a strategic plan, for implementing an operational plan that supports the strategic plan, and for the educational success and profitability of the institution. Normally, the administration is also responsible for developing the institutional budget, for reporting to the state, federal, and accrediting agencies, and for the day-to-day functioning of the institution. In many cases, the campus-level administrator is also the owner of the institution. In other cases, an individual campus may be part of a corporate chain of proprietary institutions. In this organizational structure, the campus director reports to the corporate entity.

Recruitment. The recruitment function may otherwise be known as admissions, sales, or marketing. Regardless of what it is called, the goal of this department is to attract and enroll students. Proprietary institutions have developed and used sophisticated advertisement techniques to recruit students (Simmons, 1975). Target markets and marketing areas are defined, and advertisement is initiated in a variety of media. The most prevalent recruiting vehicles include television, radio, direct mail, and high school marketing (Kleinman, 1986).

Television and radio advertisements are the most effective in penetrating the adult market. Advertising in these media has become very sophisticated. Success in radio and television advertising depends on the quality of the commercial, type of show in which the advertisement is embedded, time of the commercial, frequency of broadcast, and length of the advertisement.

High school marketing consists of sending an admissions representative to high schools to make a presentation to a group of high school students. The primary purpose is to generate occupational awareness by discussing job opportunities, descriptions, and salaries with the students. The presentation usually focuses on generic job fields, not an on individual proprietary school or its programs of study. Students express an interest in certain occupational areas by filling out a response form. The response form is turned over to recruiters for telephone follow-up. This activity requires an individual who is assigned to and responsible for coordinating the high school recruiting efforts.

Direct mail is a technique used to reach both adults and high school markets. This method consists of sending letters, cards, and brochures to prospective students.

The Higher Education Act of 1992 has altered the method by which recruitment personnel are compensated. In the past, recruiters were partially or completely compensated on the basis of enrollments they obtained. This practice of incentive compensation has been halted, and now recruiting representatives are on a salary.

Business and Finance. Initially, the finance function of proprietary institutions was confined to the establishment of typical business practices such as product pricing, accounts receivable, accounts payable, and tax preparation. While these functions still must be performed, the escalating complexity of the regulations surrounding Title IV student funding assistance requires the institution to hire personnel with expertise in credit finance. The financial aid services performed at the institutional level include (1) determining a student's eligibility for participation in the various loan and grant programs, (2) developing and explaining to the student the documentation that accompanies application for access to Title IV aid, (3) calculating and refunding the unused portion of a student's loan or grant in the event the course of study is not completed, (4) maintaining complete and accurate financial aid records, and (5) administering a loan default management program targeting all students—those who complete the program of study and those who do not. Because of federal financial aid accountability issues, the finance department's role has become much more complex and important to the economic viability of the proprietary institution.

Education. The primary functions of the education unit at most proprietary institutions are curriculum development and the delivery of the education product. Tasks associated with these functions are (1) testing prospective students for ability to benefit from exposure to the curriculum, (2) reviewing materials (for example, high school transcripts and entrance test results) and accepting or rejecting students to the program of study, (3) reviewing transcripts for the purpose of granting appropriate prior training or advanced placement credit, (4) scheduling courses based on enrollment and faculty availability, (5) hiring faculty, (6) establishing grading procedures in accordance with federal or state mandates pertaining to satisfactory progress, (7) recording and maintaining grade and attendance data, (8) maintaining the equipment used in the program of study, (9) orienting and evaluating instructors, (10) establishing employer committees to ensure the relevance of the curriculum, and (11) implementing and monitoring a program of staff development.

The primary functions in the delivery of education are similar, regardless of the type of institution. However, curriculum changes that accompany mission changes are significant. The curriculum in career colleges is beginning to look more like the curriculum found in degree-granting institutions. In fact, a number are offering degrees. In contrast, community colleges are emphasizing the economic development component of their mission, which stresses short, focused training. The convergence of mission alluded to earlier is creating a curricular convergence.

Student Services. The traditional proprietary institution centered its student services on the career placement of graduates. The success of the institution was predicated on a tight linkage between the training delivered and graduate employment. The primary role, then, of placement personnel is to locate employment for the institution's graduates. However, placement personnel also provide an array of services designed to support the achievement of this goal. Active students are exposed to a variety of career awareness activities. Such activities include inviting guest lecturers from industry to speak to the current students, administering occupational aptitude tests to help students develop career objectives, and sponsoring job fairs that are designed to bring together potential employers and students nearing completion of their course of study, as well as current students needing part-time employment.

Students receive training in successful interviewing techniques and instruction on how to create effective résumés. Career placement personnel arrange interviews with prospective employers for graduates, and they maintain frequent contact with graduates and companies that have hired them in order to monitor the appropriateness of the training and education received. Placement personnel also link the institution and the community by initiating and maintaining contact with employers for the purposes of placing graduates and current students, assisting employers with their curriculum advisory role.

Retention of students has always been a concern for proprietary institutions, but the reauthorization of the HEA in 1992 emphasizes retention as a critical indicator of quality. The reauthorization requires postsecondary institutions to maintain acceptable student retention rates as a condition of participation in Title IV programs. The State Postsecondary Review Entities (SPREs) are the mechanism established to monitor institutional retention, performance, and thirteen other standards of quality.

Additional student service activities such as orientation, student advisement, safety and security, records management, bookstore activities, community service seminars and functions, and alumni activities are usually divided among the departments listed above.

Governance Summary

The four major factors that currently differentiate the career college from the community college are profit versus public status, size, the existence of a board of trustees in community college governance, and regional accreditation. The fundamental differences in the first two are major and appear to be unaffected by current trends. However, the information in this volume suggests that the traditional distinguishing features of governing boards and accreditation standards are being eroded. States, accrediting agencies, and now the Department of Education (through the SPREs) evaluate and report retention and placement figures to prospective students. Consequently, career colleges are allocating substantial resources to the activities that promote retention and placement.

Conclusion

Proprietary schools began as autonomous business entities filling the market need for short-term, focused training. They flourished on student-paid tuition and fees before any government subsidies were available. Community colleges emerged as public education institutions serving a predominantly academic function. The G.I. Bill, amendments to the Higher Education Acts of 1972 and 1992, shifts in accreditation standards, and rapid changes in the economic climate are significant events that have altered the mission, funding, and governance of proprietary schools and community colleges. These events have been the catalysts engendering the evolution from proprietary school to career college, which is characterized by longer programs, higher academic credentials for instructors, and pursuit of accreditation and degree-granting authority. These same events have affected community colleges in a different way. Community colleges are offering more programs in partnership with the business sector that are shorter and have specific training objectives. Career colleges and community colleges have each embraced that which is traditionally perceived to be the strength of the other. This has blurred the once-stark distinction between them but has provided a broad array of delivery mechanisms for specialized postsecondary education and training.

References

Belitsky, A. H. *Private Vocational Schools and Their Students: Limited Objectives, Unlimited Opportunities.* Cambridge, Mass.: Schenkman, 1969.

Carr, D. "The Impact of Accreditation and Degree Status on Proprietary Business, Trade, and Technical Schools in New York State." Ann Arbor, Mich.: University Microfilms, 1980.

Clark, H. F., and Sloan, H. S. *Classrooms on Main Street.* New York: Teachers College Press, 1966.

Erickson, E. W., and others. *Proprietary Business Schools and Community Colleges: Resource Allocation, Student Needs, and Federal Policies.* U.S. Educational Resources Information Center, 1972. (ED 134 790)

Erwin, J. M. *The Proprietary School: Assessing Its Impact on the Collegiate Sector.* U.S. Educational Resources Information Center, 1975. (ED 145 791)

Fulton, R. A. "Proprietary Schools." In R. Ebel (ed.), *Encyclopedia of Educational Research.* (4th ed.) Toronto: Macmillan, 1969.

Katz, H. H. *A State of the Art Study of the Independent Private School Industry in the State of Illinois.* Springfield: Illinois Advisory Council on Vocational Education, 1973.

Kincaid, H. V., and Podesta, E. A. "An Exploratory Survey of Proprietary Vocational Schools." Palo Alto, Calif.: Stanford Research Institute, 1966.

Kleinman, A. "Marketing and Sales for Proprietary Schools." *Career Training,* Spring 1986.

Merisotis, J. P. (ed.). *The Changing Dimensions of Student Aid.* New Directions for Higher Education, no. 74. San Francisco: Jossey-Bass, 1991.

Shoemaker, E. A. "Community Colleges: The Challenge of Proprietary Schools." *Change,* 1973, 5 (6), 71–72,

Simmons, H. L. "A Descriptive Study of Degree Granting Proprietary Schools and Their Relationships to the Development of Community Colleges in Pennsylvania." Unpublished doctoral dissertation, Florida State University, 1975.

Tonne, H. A. *Principles of Business Education.* (2nd ed.) New York: McGraw-Hill, 1954.

JON A. HITTMAN *is director of ITT Technical Institute in Georgetown, Texas.*

The author reviews the history of proprietary schools and argues that convergence with community colleges is a possible but not a necessary direction.

The Story Behind Proprietary Schools in the United States

Craig A. Honick

In this volume, authors discuss the roles community colleges and proprietary schools will play in the United States as the twentieth century draws to a close. If community colleges are evolving into institutions primarily committed to job training, are the lines between these colleges and proprietary vocational schools becoming blurred? Is the proprietary sector, with several of its schools now offering accredited associate and bachelor's degrees, becoming a for-profit counterpart to the community college sector? Will the two be distinguishable in years to come?

Some of these questions will be answered in later chapters. Authors will define the proprietary sector as it exists today, its student population, its administrative, instructional, and financial characteristics, and its marketing and recruiting techniques. Here, the questions at hand are approached by examining the historical context in which the proprietary school developed its ethos. The evolution of the proprietary school in the United States will be examined, beginning with early proprietary educators who taught vocational as well as academic subjects in the seventeenth century.

This historical perspective will help us formulate hypotheses about how proprietary schools and community colleges may interact in years to come. We will see how the proprietary school developed its current operating principles in the context of expanding commerce—the needs of business and of students eager to enter the workforce have always driven proprietary school behavior. Conversely, the community college developed its guiding assumptions in the context of expanding educational opportunity. While the missions of the proprietary school and the community college appear now to be converging, how these two institution types behave over the next few decades may be greatly influenced by their past experiences and the equally distinctive worldviews those experiences were bound to produce.

Periods of Proprietary School Development

The proprietary school evolved through five historical periods: (1) the Colonial Era, in which entrepreneurs supplied general education as well as job skill training to students of all ages; (2) the early-to-middle nineteenth century, in which commercial school pioneers established formal schools and formal business curricula; (3) the late nineteenth century, in which the beginnings of a proprietary school sector emerge in the form of a business college alliance; (4) the early twentieth century, in which Progressive Era reformers and public vocational education advocates attacked the legitimacy of the proprietary schools, leading the sector to form its own regulatory and lobbying body to defend itself; and (5) the mid-twentieth century, in which the proprietary sector exercises its lobbying power and includes itself in federal grant and loan programs. Later in this chapter, the proprietary school's experience will be compared briefly with the emergence and development of the community college in the United States.

The Colonial Era Proprietary Schools: Original Job Training Institutions in the United States

The proprietary school can claim status as a traditional institution in the United States in the sense that it was born in the Colonial Era and has survived this nation's many social and political events intact. Research suggests that proprietary vocational schools in this country are as old as the grammar schools and colleges. In 1636, a year after the Puritans of Massachusetts founded the Boston Public Latin School and the same year they founded Harvard College, a man named James Morton was reportedly busy teaching the young people of Plymouth Colony to "cast accounts," an early form of business accounting (Haynes and Jackson, 1935).

During the Colonial Era, there were a variety of proprietary schools much like the ones we have today—surveying and navigation schools, business and commercial schools, and schools of building trades (Seyboldt, 1971). There were avocational schools that taught dance, needlework, and "ouranology" (sky-watching) (Kendall, 1973). Most were private ventures, typically run by a single instructor who had a particular skill or range of skills for sale. Some have been described as "mama and papa affairs, with the wife instructing girls in 'curious works' and the husband concentrating upon 'higher studies'" (Kendall, 1973, p. 73). They were an everyday part of colonial life, far outnumbering publicly supported schools. In colonial times, as is true today, if a skill was in demand there was likely to be an educator, or at least a business person, willing to teach others to master it. And, following the form of most business enterprises of the day, the early proprietary educators turned to advertising to compete for students. Seyboldt's (1971) research uncovered a variety of advertisements placed by private, for-profit vocational educators during the colonial period. They show that the type of competition proprietary schools face today was a real part of their environment in the colonies.

One of the earliest advertisements for a trade and technical school appeared in a March, 1709 issue of the *Boston News Letter:* "OPPosite to the Mitre Tavern in Fish-street near to Scarletts Wharf, Boston, are Taught Writing, Arithmetick in all it parts; And also Geometry, Trigonometry, Plain and Spherical, Surveying, Dialling, Gauging, Navigation, Astronomy; The Projection of the Sphere, and the use of Mathematical Instruments: By Owen Harris" (Seyboldt, 1971, p. 35).

A particularly interesting public notice in 1771, placed by a well-known builder named Thomas Nevell, reveals not only the nature of an architectural school in colonial times but shows how a proprietor might have gone about marketing his courses. Nevell, a professional architect, senses a void in the marketplace for trained architects like himself. Rather than take on apprentices who, while perhaps working for free, would take his time away from his own business at hand, he opens a school. The more apprentices, the more he must manage and the less he can do himself. By establishing a school outside of business hours and using economies of scale to maximize his own contribution (a class of six, "at least"), he will manage to earn a profit for his time and energy, charging both an entrance fee and a regular monthly fee. He promises to train a "person of common capacity" in "two months, at most" to master the "mystery" of the carpenter's business. These claims foreshadow the practice of today's schools, whereby trade schools offer to fully equip students with skills in a short period of time so as to propel them quickly and successfully into the working world.

Today's proprietary schools are known for their niche vocational programs and for their aggressive advertising campaigns on television and in print. They are also known for their instability. Proprietary schools have attracted a large number of critics throughout history because of these characteristics. In any event, many of the qualities we associate with today's proprietary schools clearly have roots in the Colonial Era.

Nineteenth Century Proprietaries Mount a National Challenge

The nation significantly expanded its industrial activity in the early nineteenth century, and businesses that were once small became large and, in some cases, far-flung. Managing apprenticeships became more difficult at the same time the demand for better-trained personnel increased (Lyon, 1922). Entrepreneurial educators saw in these trends an opportunity to attract a steady flow of vocational students.

The demand for skilled workers spurred some proprietary school owners to institutionalize their curriculum and form more permanent ties with urban centers. This led to the establishment of permanent school sites.

Formal Schools

During the 1820s and 1830s, several private business schools emerged in major eastern cities that resemble today's business colleges and that would inspire the formation of university-affiliated business schools later in the nineteenth century (Haynes and Jackson, 1935; Herrick, 1904; Lyon, 1922).

The typical business colleges in the decades just prior to the Civil War retained the flavor of the colonial schools at the same time they were pregnant with developments that would come full-term in the generation after Appomattox. They were often mobile, following the flow of the population out into the western territories (Lyon, 1922). Like their predecessors, they concentrated on teaching penmanship, bookkeeping, commercial arithmetic, commercial law, and foreign languages and were run by men who started out as "masters" in their respective fields, usually penmanship or accounting.

Notably, the first half of the nineteenth century ushered in significant changes in the structure of business education. James A. Bennett argued against the apprenticeship system "by stating that any business transaction was reducible to a regular, orderly, and systematic statement, based on a comprehension of that transaction, and that such a statement could be given to a student equally as well in the schoolroom as in the office" (Herrick, 1904, p. 18). Bennett proceeded to structure classes in his school to simulate office environments. He made records of transactions from actual or facsimile business papers and documents to introduce students to practices of the counting houses. Such developments suggest an education sector positioning itself; entrepreneurs who studied the niche that existed for business and commercial education began to develop the vehicles that would enable them to control the nature of commercial education. In the Colonial Era, masters found they had to send their apprentices to evening school in order to supplement their training with formal theory. In a departure from their predecessors, the proprietary school owners of the early nineteenth century began to see the virtues of combining the experiential nature of an apprenticeship with the theoretical foundation and consistent delivery of classroom lectures and exercises.

Before the outbreak of the Civil War, leading proprietary educators would take further steps to transform the proprietary sector from a collection of itinerant instructors to trained teachers housed in permanent schools. In 1853, H. B. Stratton and H. D. Bryant, both former students at Folsom Business College in Cleveland, formed a partnership with James W. Lusk, the Spencer penmanship schools' representative in northern Ohio, to establish the first Bryant and Stratton College. On this model, Bryant and Stratton would form partnerships in the major cities of the northeast with local proprietary school owners and develop a chain of Bryant and Stratton colleges; this was to be the nation's first "corporate" or "chain" school.

At the same time Bryant and Stratton were building their empire, George W. Eastman and his nephew, H. G. Eastman, were making names for themselves as business school proprietors—the former in Rochester; the latter, in Oswego, New York, in St. Louis, Missouri, and finally in Poughkeepsie, New York. While we know from Seyboldt (1971) that proprietary school owners had used newspaper advertising to their advantage since colonial times, H. G. Eastman is credited with elevating proprietary school advertising to a new level: "At times he would buy a whole page in the New York papers at a cost of from $1500 to $3,000. Mr. Eastman organized a full brass band which he used in various cities to gather crowds, after which the claims of his school would be presented in a stump speech, and advertising material distributed. Ornamental penmanship was similarly employed to interest people, after which they would be canvassed" (Herrick, 1904, p. 190).

Clearly, while Bryant and Stratton attempted to maximize the profit potential of their proprietary schools through franchises, Eastman found that high-profile advertising successfully sold career training. These practices would evolve still further after the Civil War.

In addition to the emergence of commercial schools, we know that proprietary medical schools saw their heyday in the nineteenth century, leading up to the Civil War (Kaufman, 1976). Nineteenth-century medical schools were set up much the same way commercial schools were. Physicians—often a group of physicians—would set up a practice in a town and would capitalize on the fact that they had an office to open small medical colleges. Kaufman (1976) explains that they were often encouraged by local townspeople because the town felt a heightened sense of prestige by having a "college" located in town.

In the nineteenth-century United States, higher education was still something to which only the elite had access. A college of any nature that provided access could potentially benefit a community. Private, for-profit medical schools would continue to operate until the Flexner Report of 1910 (Flexner, 1910), which sharply criticized the condition of medical education in the United States and Canada, marked the end of their dominance.

Proprietary Schools Following the Civil War

The proprietary sector evolved further during the "Gilded Age"—the period between the end of the Civil War and the dawn of the twentieth century—than any other time in the nation's history. Haynes and Jackson (1935) called the period between 1850 and 1890 the "period of dominance" for private business education (p. 32). Industrial expansion fueled business sector growth to which the proprietary school responded. According to James (c1904), commercial schools alone increased from fewer than a dozen with about 30 teachers and

1,000 pupils in the 1850s to 341 schools with 1,764 instructors and 77,746 students, 82 percent being in day classes, in the late 1890s (in Lyon, 1922, p. 273). Haynes and Jackson (1935) cited Bureau of Education figures placing the number of students in business colleges alone at 115,748 in 1893 (p. 36).

James (c1904) noted other changes: "Increased popularity led to higher fees, longer courses, to the preparation of printed texts; life and interchangeable scholarships were abolished; the teaching force was increased; students were no longer adults wearied by day labor; the commercial school began to draw young men and boys looking forward to employment; day classes largely took place of evening instruction; school equipment improved and gradually these institutions grew into the permanent place in public favor which they enjoy today" (Lyon, 1922, pp. 272–273).

This era also saw the introduction of the Remington Model 1 typewriter, an invention with profound potential for transforming the workplace but one that would require new and extensive training. The calculator and the stenographic machine were also inventions that represented profound changes to the office and that necessitated trained operators. The Gregg shorthand method (a method still taught today) was introduced by its namesake, John Robert Gregg.

During this period, we see the development of a true sector, anchored by the success of the business colleges. Here, all of the signs of an emerging sector were born. The period saw the first professional association of proprietary schools, along with the first attempts at self-regulation. It also saw the first motions on the part of the proprietary sector to establish government relations. And finally, the persistent efforts of the business school leadership led to the formation of the business education section of the National Education Association.

First Attempts at Self-Regulation. The beginnings of an industry-wide association of business schools grew out of the Bryant-Stratton chain, by far the most dominant alliance of proprietary schools at the time, with more than fifty business colleges in several major cities. After a disagreement with Bryant and Stratton over policy, several school owners split off from the Bryant-Stratton group in 1865 to form the National Union of Business Colleges (NUBC). The NUBC appears to have been the first formal and cooperative attempt within the sector to reform the sector itself. At their meeting in 1866, the NUBC leaders announced their intentions to systematize their methods of instruction and discourage the idea that a business education could be obtained in a few weeks.

NUBC was short-lived, however, as Bryant and Stratton made the necessary concessions to bring the rebellious partners back into the fold by 1866 and formed the International Association of Business Colleges to supersede the NUBC. The self-reform movement lived on, however, as most of the prominent schools made efforts to lengthen their courses and shore up curricula (Herrick, 1904, p. 198). This suggests that the public had expressed its discontent with the practices of some of the schools; however, the extent of this discontent is not clear.

Competition. It appears that for more than two centuries the private, for-profit vocational school operated in a market of its own, virtually untouched by other educational sectors. By 1890, however, momentum had grown in the nation to adapt public school programs to address the expanding needs of industry. While scattered bookkeeping, commercial arithmetic, penmanship, and typing classes existed in public high schools from the 1850s, it was not until the last decade of the nineteenth century that the nation's first public commercial secondary school—the Washington Commercial High School in the District of Columbia—was established. Petrello (1988) argues that the competition from these schools did not faze the career school industry. Perhaps not, but the competition that proprietary schools would receive in the twentieth century, while it would not deter the growth of the for-profit sector, would cast them in a different light before the public. The schools would come under the intense scrutiny of Progressive reformers and would be forced to play second fiddle to newly established public vocational schools and vocational programs in public high schools.

Twentieth Century: The Public Redefines the Private, For-Profit School

Perhaps the most significant development to affect proprietary education in the United States was the shift in public perception that took place at the onset of the twentieth century. This shift is reflected in a speech given by William C. Redfield, the Secretary of Commerce in 1913, before the National Society for the Promotion of Industrial Education (NSPIE): "Let me suggest that while we must not forget the great debt we owe to the private vocational schools, the future of this education lies in the hands of the public school. The private industrial schools have been the beacons which have lighted the course on which the ship of state must now sail" (NSPIE, 1913).

The Progressive Era would leave its mark on the proprietary sector. It was during this period, from the dawn of the 1900s through the 1920s, that Congress and the state legislatures passed a flood of reform legislation designed to clean up industry, government, and education. In 1902, Oregon became the first state to adopt the use of the initiative and referendum. Congress passed the Food and Drug Act, the Meat Inspection Act, the Sherman Antitrust Act, and several wage and child labor laws. Proprietary schools meanwhile, outside government control, catered heavily to less-educated, blue-collar families, and affected many young Americans; the schools could not find shelter from the hailstorm of reform legislation and progressive government.

The private, for-profit vocational school would be pushed to the penumbra of postsecondary education in the United States. As mentioned earlier, among the proprietary schools of the Colonial Era were illegitimate operators who seized upon unsuspecting and eager students. The sector also came together to battle criticism in the late nineteenth century. It is during the early twentieth century, the Progressive Era, however, that the schools' reputation for aggressive solicitation of students, misleading advertising, and inadequate curricula would solidify in the minds of their critics.

Sources of Attacks

Against this backdrop of new competition from state agencies and scrutiny on the part of determined Progressives, for-profit schools came under fire from those eager to reform the nation's vocational education system. Minutes of meetings conducted by NSPIE, and reports such as one produced by the City Club of Chicago in 1912, reveal that detractors of proprietary schools were drawn heavily from public education, industry, and labor (City Club of Chicago, 1912; NSPIE, 1907, 1908, 1910, 1911, 1913).

Public school educators and those who advocated federal support for vocational programs in the public schools found three major problems with the for-profit schools. First, and perhaps foremost, was what they considered to be the unscrupulous recruitment of young students through misleading advertisements and smooth-talking personal representatives. Detractors attributed these practices directly to the keen competition among schools in a unregulated marketplace and their profit motive.

The problem many educators had with the competition among profit-driven schools raises yet another issue that specifically affected the private commercial schools in the late nineteenth and early twentieth centuries. The appeal of a "white collar and cuffs and clean clothes"—which suggests that the lure of office work, if only clerical, was more closely linked with professional status than manual labor—had become a hot selling item for private commercial schools since the expansion of business activity in the late nineteenth century. Vocational education advocates accused for-profit vocational schools of misleading some students about their chances for employment and of diverting many young boys and girls into career training that would not benefit them as much as would learning a trade. This is similar to the "ability to benefit" issue surrounding proprietary school recruitment today.

A committee under the sponsorship of the City Club of Chicago in 1912 looked into private vocational schools along with a number of other types of vocational programs and included the following in their report:

> Most of the solicitors for these schools are working on a commission basis and tend, therefore, to be more interested in securing the students than they are in telling the truth; in the amount of business they secure than in the maturity or fitness of the pupils they solicit. In very many cases the pupils, even from the fifth grade and up, are induced to leave the public schools for the purpose of taking a course in some business college. Pupils are solicited who have no adaptability for commercial training.
>
> Many students are secured by means of what must be regarded as misrepresentation on the part of the solicitor. They promise the prospective student a job at the end of his short term of study. They draw attention to the fact that cer-

tain students have completed courses of study in a short period of time and are now holding good positions. Some of them who enroll have sufficient native ability or have received such previous training that they are enabled to complete the work in the promised time and hold a job when secured. The solicitor uses these examples as a bait to catch others who have not these qualifications. No guarantee is given that the student will be able to hold a position, and many take places only to lose them because they are incompetent. [City Club of Chicago, 1912, pp. 253–254]

This type of scrutiny, as we shall see, recurs throughout the twentieth century.

Attacks from Labor Representatives. Labor groups had other reasons for disliking the schools. Their distrust stemmed from their belief that the proprietary vocational schools, specifically trade schools, served to provide fodder for industrialists bent on breaking worker strikes. Critics from labor also believed that for-profit trade schools, with their short courses, diluted the prestige and quality of the trades.

It is difficult to determine how much of labor's opposition came from actual experience with graduates of these schools or from the natural bias one would expect trained craftsmen to have against those trained outside the guild. We can also empathize with their distrust of employers' support of certain trade schools, as organized labor had many run-ins with strikebreakers beginning the late 1800s. However, we must be cautious about completely accepting the inflammatory statements that brand such schools as "scab hatcheries." In truth, as reports from both Chicago (City Club of Chicago, 1912) and New York (Public Education Committee, 1918, in Lyon, 1922) indicate, nonprofit private schools as well as public programs offered courses that were not much longer and, in some cases, were shorter than some for-profit institutions. Labor interests led them to call for public industrial education under the conditions that it be of the "right kind" (City Club of Chicago, 1912, p. 73).

Nevertheless, labor's unabashed condemnation of private, for-profit trade schools formed one more flank in the crusade a large segment of society had launched against the proprietary sector. When organized labor and public educators can unite in their dislike for an institution, it does not bode well for the institution. When organized labor and manufacturing interests can agree, it had better brace for tough times ahead. In the case of the proprietary sector, that is exactly what happened.

Attacks from Industry and Businessmen. Many manufacturers of the day, particularly those aligned with NSPIE and the National Association of Manufacturers, pushed for the Smith-Hughes Act of 1917, which, in effect, would dilute the competitive position of proprietary schools. Big business stood to benefit from a tax-supported vocational education program that would train workers. In addition, industry felt that control over public instruction offered it more influence in society than backing a loose affiliation of private schools.

Effects of Progressive Era Attacks on Proprietary Schools

As is the case in most industries, especially deregulated industries, a few operators can cast an image that will tarnish the image of an entire group. In the case of proprietary schools during this period, it is likely that the established, reputable schools suffered as a result of other, less reputable operators.

The experience proprietary schools endured through the early part of the twentieth century would permanently set the sector against the nation's public education system. The proprietary sector would continue to have to fight for respectability and acceptance. This created an incentive for the sector's first lasting trade association, the National Association of Accredited Commercial Schools (NAACS).

It was no coincidence, perhaps, that NAACS was founded in Chicago in December, 1912, (Petrello, 1988) just ten months after the Report on Vocational Training was submitted to the City Club of Chicago by its special committee. By 1920, NAACS had a code of ethics that addressed the attacks it had been receiving from labor, educators, industry, and the public at large. The code set strict guidelines for professional conduct. NAACS, according to Petrello (1988), would also use the consolidated power of the proprietary sector to lobby the national government.

The Modern Era: Government Support and Regulation

The Servicemen's Readjustment Act (G.I. Bill) passed in 1944 was a package of benefits conceived to support servicemen who wished to seek education after their tours of duty, along with other assistance such as home and business loans, retirement pay, and job counseling (U.S. War Department, 1944). Approved proprietary schools were included in the list of schools that a returning service person could attend and for which he or she could be reimbursed. In fact, during the first few years of the program, a veteran could pursue a wide variety of avocational as well as vocational courses and be reimbursed up to a specified amount.

This was the first time that for-profit schools received a significant federal subsidy, albeit by way of individuals; it ushered in a new era for the schools as it shifted the environment from one that forced the schools to be purely market-driven to one that allowed them to be partially federally subsidized. It also opened the door to a new way the schools could get into trouble. Here, we see the beginnings of behavior that would repeat itself after 1972 when some proprietary schools were to be included in federal grant and federally guaranteed student loan programs: schools eligible for G.I. Bill students set their rates to the maximum amount the government would pay—more often than not, rates that were unrelated to actual costs. They also had incentives from the government to recruit students regardless of their ability to benefit from the school's instruction.

The G.I. Bill education program was virtually wide open when it began. Under the 1944 G.I. Bill, just about any veteran could enter any kind of program for any reason for just about any period of time and get reimbursed for it. Schools of all types, but particularly for-profit schools used to marketing aggressively, vied for returning veterans and employed unusual techniques to attract them. A whole crop of new schools emerged on the scene to get a slice of the federal fund pie.

Participation by Proprietary Schools. The G.I. Bill was a boon for private, for-profit vocational schools. Lee and Merisotis (1990) report that proprietary schools served more students on the G.I. Bill than any other institutional type.

The Government Accounting Office (GAO) report also establishes that more than 600,000 veterans were enrolled in privately operated trade schools in 1949, a figure that dropped to 283,000 in late 1950 (p. 82). More than 1,677,000 veterans attended private trade schools under the 1944 provisions of the G.I. Bill, 20 percent of them reportedly completing their courses (p. 81). The report also notes the importance of trade schools to the economy, asserting that "trades and industrial occupations offer employment to about 40 percent of the working population of the country" (p. 81). On the downside, the report concludes that 65 percent of the for-profit schools studied disclosed questionable practices that resulted in excessive charges to the Treasury (p. 110). A closer look at the alleged excessive charges revealed that in many cases Veterans Administration (VA) representatives were involved in fraud and deception. The VA admitted the tracking system for training and funding was seriously flawed (U.S. Congress, 1951).

Fallout. While the VA officially took the brunt of the scandal surrounding the G.I. Bill affair, the proprietary sector did not emerge from this period unscathed. The sector experienced an infusion of new capital in the form of loosely regulated government subsidies that fed the growth of opportunistic schools. The sector now, more than ever, was affected by public policies fostering the growth of illegitimate operators within the sector. While Petrello (1988) points out that including the for-profit sector in the government program elevated the for-profits' prestige, the G.I. Bill experience also made very public the potential for-profits could have for putting profit ahead of education. On balance, the proprietary sector came away tarnished. While restrictions were tightened up for G.I. Bill provisions following the Korean and Vietnam Wars, the reverberations of scandal following World War II can still be felt today. The same potential for scandal is embodied in the sector's reaction to the amendments to the HEA of 1972, which included accredited proprietary schools on the list of schools to which students could direct their federally guaranteed student loans.

Growth into the Twentieth Century. The proprietary schools were weakened in the early part of the twentieth century, but they were poised to grow strong as a result of their experience. Ironically, as public community colleges began to grow, proprietary schools flourished alongside them. They have continued to grow since World War II, with a surge in the 1970s and 1980s in response to their inclusion in federally guaranteed student loan programs (Lee and Merisotis, 1990). Today, the sector is strong and diverse.

The history of the proprietary school in the United States shows that, from colonial times, it developed to fill a vacuum in education and training. In response to the growth of American industry and changes in the structure of American business, it evolved from a group of itinerant instructors scattered around the nation's major cities into established schools and, in some case, chains of schools. The private vocational school continued to seek out pockets in the market once the public school system grew to challenge it. In the twentieth century, the school survived competition from other educational and training institutions and attacks from those who looked askance at their entrepreneurial tactics. The proprietary school made inroads into the overall postsecondary sector when it fought its way into federal grant and loan programs, first with the G.I. Bill and later with its inclusion in the amendments to the HEA of 1972 and 1986.

In Contrast: The Community College

In stark contrast to the origin and development of the nation's proprietary schools, the community college was born in the late nineteenth and early twentieth centuries as a "junior college," a preparatory unit that would prepare college students for their second two years of course work. It was an academic institution primarily and, instead of pioneering in a free market, it was subordinated to the elite universities that controlled its sector (Brint and Karabel, 1989; Cohen and Brawer, 1989). The growth of the community college sector paralleled the growth of the proprietary sector in the twentieth century. Both profited greatly from the G.I. Bill, and both diversified their offerings under the HEA and the Job Training Partnership Act (JTPA) (Brint and Karabel, 1989; Cohen and Brawer, 1989; Lee and Merisotis, 1990.)

The community colleges expanded their vocational programs after World War II and accelerated their drive toward vocationalism in the 1970s. According to Brint and Karabel (1989), community college leaders made the decision in the early 1970s to pursue job training more voraciously than the transfer function as a matter of survival. They felt that job training markets left untouched by universities and four-year colleges represented a means by which these leaders could strike out and establish autonomy. Without this niche and the independence it represented, the community college would continue to be subject to the whims of the more dominant institutions of higher education. Cohen and Brawer (1989) argued that the community college began to change after World War II, largely in response to the characteristics of a new cadre of students less inclined toward a liberal education and more directed toward the job market. They added that community colleges, in response to the changing demands of its students, did not suffer the same "goal displacement" that other higher education institutions did; their goals, the authors claimed, have always been tied to student demand (pp. 22–23). Whether the impetus for change in the community college has been driven primarily by foresight on the part of its leaders or by the inertia of its student body, the institution type has nevertheless operated under both the benefits and the constraints of public resources and public demands.

Conclusion

Proprietary schools and community colleges in the United States developed within very different contexts for most of their histories. Their origin and experience may explain why, to extend Clowes's metaphor presented in Chapter One, the community college now lives in small villages near the castle proper—albeit outside the walls—and the proprietary school finds itself in the hinterlands of higher education. While the soil is less fertile and the territory less secure the farther one travels from the castle keep, the breeze flows more freely and the people are less encumbered by the rules and customs of the kingdom.

The proprietary school was born as a free-market business enterprise; the community college as a unit subordinate to powerful private and state-run masters. The proprietary school is therefore comfortable dwelling on the penumbra of higher education, while it is known to travel into the kingdom occasionally to gather what riches it can. As some proprietary schools venture near the castle walls to take advantage of the programs the state offers, they may find themselves getting increasingly comfortable, settling down, assimilating among the villagers.

So too, as some community colleges feel increasingly stifled by life in the shadow of the castle walls and attempt to venture to the outskirts of the kingdom, they may find themselves without roots, struggling to feel their way through an undefined landscape. They may prosper. They may suffer. The yet unwritten chapters of history will tell if community colleges are "proprietary" enough or, conversely, if proprietary schools are "community" enough by nature to meet the challenges of change.

References

Brint, S., and Karabel, J. *The Diverted Dream: Community Colleges and the Promise of Educational Opportunity in America, 1900–1985.* New York: Oxford University Press, 1989.

City Club of Chicago. *A Report on Vocational Training in Chicago and in Other Cities.* Chicago: City Club of Chicago, 1912.

Cohen, A., and Brawer, F. *The American Community College.* (2nd ed.) San Francisco: Jossey-Bass, 1989.

Flexner, A. *Medical Education in the United States and Canada: A Report to the Carnegie Foundation for the Advancement of Teaching.* New York: Ayer, 1910.

Haynes, B. R., and Jackson, H. P. *A History of Business Education in the United States.* Cincinnati, Ohio: South-Western, 1935.

Herrick, C. A. *Meaning and Practice of Commercial Education.* New York: Macmillan, 1904.

James, E. J. *Commercial Education. Monographs on Education in the United States.* New York: Lyon, c1904.

Kaufman, M. *American Medical Education: The Formative Years, 1765–1910*. Westport, Conn.: Greenwood Press, 1976.

Kendall, K. "Beyond Mother's Knee." *American Heritage*, June 1973.

Lee, J. B., and Merisotis, J. P. *Proprietary Schools: Programs, Policies, and Prospects*. ASHE-ERIC Higher Education Report No. 5. Washington, D.C.: George Washington University, School of Education and Human Development, 1990. (ED 331 337)

Lyon, L. S. *Education for Business*. Chicago: University of Chicago Press, 1922.

National Society for the Promotion of Industrial Education (NSPIE). *Bulletin No. 3: Symposium on Industrial Education*. New York: National Society for the Promotion of Industrial Education, 1907.

National Society for the Promotion of Industrial Education (NSPIE). *Bulletin No. 6: Proceedings of First Annual Meeting, Chicago*. Part 2. New York: National Society for the Promotion of Industrial Education, 1908.

National Society for the Promotion of Industrial Education (NSPIE). *Bulletin No. 10: Proceedings of Third Annual Meeting, Milwaukee*. New York: National Society for the Promotion of Industrial Education, 1910.

National Society for the Promotion of Industrial Education (NSPIE). *Proceedings of Fourth Annual Meeting*. New York: National Society for the Promotion of Industrial Education, 1911.

National Society for the Promotion of Industrial Education (NSPIE). *Proceedings of Sixth Annual Meeting*. New York: National Society for the Promotion of Industrial Education, 1913.

Petrello, G. J. *In Service to America: AICS at 75*. New York: McGraw-Hill, 1988.

Seyboldt, R. F. *Source Studies in American Colonial Education: The Private School*. New York: Arno Press and *New York Times*, 1971.

U.S. Congress. *House Select Committee to Investigate Educational and Training Program Under GI Bill*. Washington, D.C.: U.S. Government Printing Office, 1951.

U.S. General Accounting Office. *General Accounting Office Report of Survey, Veterans' Education and Training Program: Report by the Chief of Investigations of a Survey of the Veterans Administration Relating to Education and Training Under the Act of 1944, known as "The GI Bill of Rights."* Washington, D.C.: U.S. Government Printing Office, 1951.

U.S. War Department. *Explanation of the Provisions of "The GI Bill of Rights."* War Department pamphlet no. 21–24. Washington, D.C.: U.S. Government Printing Office, 1944.

CRAIG A. HONICK *is a doctoral student in the Higher Education and Organizational Change Division of the Graduate School of Education and Information Studies, University of California, Los Angeles.*

The curricula of career and community colleges are changing, and the direction of change is toward convergence.

Curriculum as a Path to Convergence

Cheryl Hyslop, Michael H. Parsons

The twentieth century is ending. Its last decade has been one of transformational change. Curriculum change—the driving force in higher education—makes the process apparent.

Curriculum revision as an agent of change is not new. In 1977, the Carnegie Foundation for the Advancement of Teaching reviewed college curricula. Three areas received attention because of accelerated rates of change—the enhancement of basic skills, the establishment of connections with the world of work, and the encouragement of moral values (Stadtman, 1977). Colleges were encouraged to implement modifications in response to societal need.

What has occurred in these past eighteen years? Curriculum reform was the focus of the Winter 1994 issue of the *Educational Record*. The authors of this volume restate the old challenge: Young (1994) suggests that "we . . . need to educate men and women not only to pursue their own personal interests, but also to fulfill their social and civic obligations" (p. 11); Weingartner (1994) delineates the need for proficiency in reading, speaking, mathematics applications, and critical thinking; and Gaudiani defines the new curriculum as a means of addressing urgent challenges posed by a changing world.

Two-year colleges, however, have functioned somewhat differently than the other sectors of higher education. The Institute for Future Studies at Macomb Community College in Michigan, for example, regularly assesses the social context in which the "people's colleges" operate. Banach and Lorenzo (1993) describe the process: "In an age which is characterized by radical change, the emphasis must shift to the process—planning and thinking strategically. To effectively manage in an era of uncertainty, the process can never stop" (p. 37). Who is meeting the challenge presented by the need to manage change in the two-year sector?

Recently, much has been written regarding the diversity of the institutions embracing change. Career colleges, technical colleges, proprietary institutions, and corporate classrooms (Eurich, 1985) seem to be joining with public, comprehensive community colleges in contributing to societal reform and renewal.

Is the foregoing more than a perception? Brand (1993) suggests that educators package knowledge for administrative convenience and have been doing it for so long that the process is sometimes perceived as a law of nature. Society needs material presented in a concise, focused way that prepares students for the challenges presented by the world of work. Morris suggests that career colleges offer an alternative for those seeking marketable skills for immediate job entry. "These schools, usually small in comparison to conventional colleges . . . seem able to adapt efficiently to the ever-changing demands of potential employers and to student bodies of varying ethnic, cultural and socioeconomic composition" (Morris, 1993, p. 22). How unique is his perception?

The League for Innovation in the Community College received information from 748 community colleges regarding workforce training. The responses suggested that "community colleges represent an installed base resource with the capability—and, it appears, the inclination—to provide the workforce training most needed by the nation's economy" (Doucette, 1993, p. 18). The League study reveals that community colleges are responding to change management in a manner similar to that of the career colleges. The process has come full circle. Curriculum in the community and career college sectors seems to be on a convergence course.

What are the results of the convergence likely to be? We sought an answer by identifying an analytical paradigm and conducting a pilot survey. The results have been synthesized into a description of the nature of curriculum convergence in community and career colleges.

Curriculum Renaissance: The Ascending Spiral

A series of studies on trends in curriculum innovation over the last five years suggest a common theme. There has been a gradual shift from fragmentation to integration and coherence. Shaw (1989) describes the process as an ascending spiral. She proposes that while the movement of a spiral is circular, it should not be confused with a pendulum that repeatedly passes over the same area. "A spiral covers the same territory in a new context, on a new and different plane, with each pass, and thus affords abundant possibilities for new combinations" (p. 24). To grasp the nature of curriculum innovation, one must examine the context in which the spiral occurs and seek out the symbiotic relationships between individual units of change and the direction of the spiral. The Shaw paradigm is based on a series of empirical indicators that are useful for pinpointing areas of similarity and difference between institutional genres. These indicators provide the focus for our analysis and include general education, curriculum structure, developmental education, technical specialization, and curriculum connectors.

Pilot Survey

Shaw's indicators served as a structure for gathering empirical data. The purpose of conducting the survey was to integrate theory and practice.

The design of the survey was impressionistic rather than scientific. The participants were selected because of their diversity, longevity, and accessibility. Careful attention was given to including comprehensive and specialized institutions. The results of the survey provide empirical support for the Shaw paradigm.

Included in the survey were business colleges and technical institutions in Florida, Maryland, Michigan, and New York. Further, comprehensive studies of technical institutions in California and Georgia were reviewed to lend perspective. Concurrently, an assessment of community college curriculum trends as presented in national literature lent comparative insight. This volume's metaphorical framework emerged as one of convergence rather than divergence.

Shaw Paradigm

The core of curriculum assessment resides in providing a meaningful general education for a very diverse student body (Dever and Templin, 1994). Shaw suggests that the focus should be on what every graduate of the community college must know. A quality assurance manual published by the Association of Independent Colleges and Schools (AICS) agrees that "employees and faculty have a strong interest in the attitudes, values, and behaviors of graduates. [We] believe that curricula . . . should change to include more attention to those areas . . ." (Harris, Hillenmeyer, and Foran, 1989, p. 27). All of the institutions examined reflected this position. Hagerstown Business College, for example, requires a minimum of twenty-one credits in general education as a component of earning the associate degree (Hagerstown Business College, 1991). Twenty credits is the minimum requirement for all associate degrees in the Code of Maryland Regulations for public community colleges (Code of Maryland Regulations, 1990). In Florida, the Florida Career Institute adopted a comprehensive general education program in preparation for awarding the associate degree and becoming the Southwest Florida College of Business (personal communication, 1992).

Shaw suggests that many curriculum models address the general education function. She is supported by Lorenzo and Armes-LeCroy (1994). They present a ten-point framework for initiating fundamental change in the community college. For general education, they emphasize outputs—"measures of quality, relevancy, utility, responsiveness, and value" (p. 18). The emergence of quality assessment programs in both genres reinforces the hallmark of convergence.

The next facet of the Shaw paradigm is curriculum structure. It describes what the curriculum expects of the student and requires a broad focus so that it is possible to incorporate varied learning styles. Recently, several studies have examined structure and what has been identified by Thompson as a "cooperative paradox" is evident among the institutions surveyed.

According to Thompson (1994), a cooperative paradox is one where a design based on technical proficiency and expertise is developed with the cooperation of several contributors from area technical schools, technical institutes, and comprehensive community colleges in close alignment with the industrial sector. Adapting to the environment entails reexamining the traditional packaging of courses and experimenting with modularized instruction, distance learning, weekend colleges, and on-site learning in business or industry.

Examples of cooperative endeavors include Baker College in Muskegon, Michigan. Baker College worked with the Michigan Economic Development Corporation, the Michigan Economic Growth Alliance, and Muskegon Community College in developing health care training programs, computer offerings, and child care development services. These actions were initiated in partnership with the public community college and were funded, in part, through a public bond issue. The focus was cooperative planning to achieve economic viability (Jewel, 1993).

Berkeley College, a two-year, private institution in White Plains, New York, that is authorized to award associate degrees is experiencing a situation similar to Baker College. "As changes occur in the professional marketplace, Berkeley must continue to adapt its programs and instructional methods to continue to produce an employable graduate. As more Berkeley graduates express interest in pursuing baccalaureate degrees, the college must continue to develop articulation agreements with four year colleges that will allow for easy transfer of credit" (Burke, 1994, p. 37).

Berkeley has horizontal agreements with public community colleges and vertical ones with four-year institutions. Further, there are alliances with private sector associations designed to create career paths that meet employment needs in Westchester, Putnam, and Rockland Counties. Overall, the college has become an integral partner in a tri-county economic development effort.

Similar examples could be drawn from all institutions surveyed. In essence, alignment emerged as a synthesis among public and private two-year colleges, four-year colleges, and the business-industry sector. Shaw's insight and the paradox were in accord.

The third unit in Shaw's paradigm is developmental education—or curriculum boundary spanners used to assist students in progressing up the vertical curriculum axis. All of the institutions surveyed offered a developmental program. It was useful to compare one of them with a study of several California career colleges. MoTech Education Centers is headquartered in Livonia, Michigan. They have a central campus, an extended education facility, and scattered sites in Michigan and other states. They train personnel for selected technologies in the automobile industry. Recently, they found it necessary to institute developmental programs. After consultation with industry representatives, Center staff built the program around applied skills. Examples included in reading and mathematics courses were drawn from on-the-job experiences students were likely to encounter upon employment. The real-world focus helped students understand the material in a context that was relevant to them. As a result, retention increased within the institutions (personal communication, 1992). The process described has been labeled contextual learning. Hull points out that the Community College of Rhode Island, for example, is modifying curricula to include applied concepts and recruiting teachers who practice these types of techniques (Hull, 1993).

Morris interviewed students enrolled at three inner-city Los Angeles proprietary business schools. He described the learning environment of these schools as paternalistic and reported that the interviewees were accepting of the conditions as a necessary aspect of their occupational training. The students reported that they enrolled to develop the minimal skills required to gain employment or find a better job. Placement rates were high, and interviewees seemed to understand the need for English, mathematics, and social studies development as part of the preparation process. Morris (1993) concludes: "It may be argued that many, if not the majority, of the students sampled . . . never would have attended a community or conventional college" (p. 27).

Lorenzo and Armes-LeCroy (1994) suggest that community colleges need to assure a dynamic curriculum with content continually adjusted to reflect student and marketplace needs. Career institutions share the requirement of meeting student and workforce needs.

The fourth element in Shaw's paradigm is a technical specialization. She indicates that business and industry are inextricably involved with education. Change in one necessitates a similar change in the other. Further, what is learned cannot be separated from how it is learned. In other words, technology now demands integration of method and content.

Dever and Templin (1994) provide community college applications. First, they underscore the importance of learning partnerships based on the "tech-prep" movement. Included were application of basic academic concepts to technical and other work-related contexts, on-site faculty and student internships, and school-to-work opportunities. Also, the implementation of the Secretary's Commission on Achieving Necessary Skills (SCANS) report will produce "the higher-order skills required for productivity in the twenty-first century" (p. 33). The report states that more than 1,000 community colleges are cooperating with approximately 2,500 school districts nationally to design tech-prep opportunities (Dever and Templin, 1994). Several examples are germane.

Hagerstown Business College, Hagerstown Junior College, and the Washington County Board of Education, Maryland, make up a cooperative tech-prep consortium. Seven curriculum paths are being developed jointly. Blended instruction is based on SCANS skills and career paths. A joint career development program is shared among all members, and seven environmental scans have been completed to ensure congruence between school-based learning and job requirements. Faculty and students are participating in business-industry internships designed to ensure that what is learned and how it is learned are germane to business and industry (Maryland State Department of Education, 1993–94).

Another example is the Instructor Academy sponsored by the Georgia Department of Technical and Adult Education. The academy serves the state's technical institutes. First, the department established statewide program-specific standards and curricula that reflected current job practices. The standards were developed by industry representatives, members of state agencies, and technical institute instructors. The department strongly supported the process by guaranteeing the competencies of the graduates of Georgia's technical programs. The academy provided professional development opportunities for technical institute instructors in technical skills, pedagogy, and professional upgrade (Askins and Galloy, 1993).

These examples reflect Shaw's integration of technology and learning. All postsecondary institutions face the need to develop processes that upgrade curricula. Lorenzo and Armes-LeCroy (1994) describe continuous updating and strengthening of institutional culture as a part of organizational learning.

The last facet of Shaw's paradigm is curriculum connectors. These elements integrate basic learning processes and technology. Curriculum spanning efforts based on internal and external partnerships allow educators to become involved in the information revolution.

The process of curriculum connecting is present in partnerships operating in the institutions surveyed. The Baker College partnership in Muskegon, Michigan, includes the development of a technologically current library and computer center. These facilities, funded in part with public resources, made possible the connections required if the training needs of the community, which were projected to expand over time, were to be met.

Berkeley College used an integrated, tripartite process to fashion curriculum connections. The first is computer linkages. Programs including paralegal studies, professional sales, and international marketing shared remote data bases. Students have access to the current information needed for successful career development. Second, work-study options in cooperation with business and industry allowed students to develop a realistic view of the level of performance expected by employees and the evaluative standards currently in practice. Finally, the use of field trips and enrichment visits to nearby urban centers allowed students to observe, first-hand, professional environments and interact with successful practitioners. The result of these opportunities is that graduates have the skills needed for successful transfer or employment.

Shaw concludes the presentation of her paradigm by assessing the status of one dimension of the mission shared by community and career colleges—access and excellence. "The best of these innovations is helping the curriculum bring meaning to the excellence that gives access its value" (p. 44). The five elements of the paradigm—general education, curriculum structure, developmental education, technical specialization, and curriculum connectors—emerge from our research as a convergence strategy that is valid empirically. How does the strategy relate to the metaphor that gave impetus to this volume?

Conclusion

The metaphor used to develop this volume is an interesting characterization of the process of analogy. The image of "barbarian hordes doing battle before the walls" is as elegant and as inexact as the permanence of the Berlin Wall. Yet it provides insight into the relationship between the curricula of career and community colleges.

Shaw's description of the curriculum as a spiral requires analysis. A spiral moves in a direction propelled by identifiable organic forces. What are the forces propelling curriculum convergence?

Johnstone suggests that Americans preparing for the twenty-first century are less concerned with traditional degrees and are more focused on achieving specific competencies and having them validated. Further, he perceives technology as a continuous force for decentralizing and individualizing learning (Johnstone, 1993).

Direction appears to be emerging for the spiral. All post–high school education must become more focused. Productivity is a goal; educate students in less time, at less cost, and with better results. The process will require revised models operating in alliance with emerging technologies and new partners.

Secretary of Labor, Robert Reich, proposes: "Educators, as partners in our initiatives, need to work closely with employees and workers to develop an understanding of what kind of skills employers require in their workers and what kind of jobs are available in the local labor market. Each partner . . . must take the time to develop a clear, *shared* vision of goals, and each must be particularly sensitive to the others' individual objectives" (Reich, 1993, p. 23). Failure to do so will result in ebbing national prosperity and a gradual decline into mediocrity.

A quote from AICS on career and community college curriculum change is promising:

> Perhaps the greatest opportunity for innovation in a private career school rests with its ability to develop new markets. . . . Innovation and problem solving become a passion for all people in the school, for a comfort level exists which allows for risk-taking without fear of reprisal or condemnation. . . .
>
> In order to provide quality private career education to those students who put their trust in our institutions, we must make such leadership common currency. Our forefathers, 'edupreneurs,' if you will, have left a legacy which vividly demonstrates the viability of mixing good business practices with delivering a quality educational product, consistent with making a profit." [Harris, Hillenmeyer, and Foran, 1989, pp. 67–68]

The changing direction of American postsecondary education suggests a common arena of understanding. On the day this chapter was completed, the community college author participated in a community planning forum focusing on the development of a Local Partnership Implementation Group for school-to-work opportunities. Present were business, industry, labor, and economic development leaders from the college's service area. More importantly, the local school superintendent, community college president, and the president of the local career college were also there. All participants made a commitment to modify curricula, implement work-based learning, and share resources for the development of a quality workforce for the twenty-first century.

Is this too optimistic? In building a paradigm for disseminating teaching-learning innovations, Roueche and Roueche (1994) indicate that "Good ideas are disseminated best, at least initially, among friends. The network with the greatest chance of survival is the one that occurs among individuals who seek new sources of information and who trust the sources of that information" (p. 42).

The partnerships identified by the authors are based on the type of trust described by Roueche and Roueche. They use curriculum change as a tool for societal renewal. The forces of democracy, individual achievement, and human rights were too powerful to be resisted by totalitarian systems; the Berlin Wall fell. So it is, we believe, today.

Educational partnerships for societal renewal are a force whose time has come. The Roueches suggest that the best way to improve is to examine the best models that exist. "And we have learned that the models [available] and the creative spinoffs they foster are critical to the development of more successful programs for the increasing diversity in our student populations" (Roueche and Roueche, 1994, p. 42). The noise in the background is not "moats snapping shut" but curriculum reformers chipping away at the divergence between career and community college curricula.

References

Askins, K. B., and Galloy, M. J. "A Quality Initiative for Postsecondary Technical Instructors." *Community College Journal of Research and Practice,* 1993, 17 (6), 509–518.

Banach, W. J., and Lorenzo, A. L. *Toward a New Model for Thinking and Planning: The Emerging Context for Life in America.* Warren, Mich.: Institute for Future Studies, Macomb Community College, 1993.

Brand, M. "The Challenge to Change: Reforming Higher Education." *Educational Record,* 1993, 74 (4), 6–13.

Burke, C. (ed.). *Reaccreditation Report: Middle States Association of Colleges and Schools, 1994.* White Plains, N.Y.: Berkeley College, 1994.

Code of Maryland Regulations. "Title 13B: Minimum Requirements for Associate Degree Granting Institutions." Annapolis: Maryland Higher Education Commission, 1990.

Dever, J. T., and Templin, R. G. "Assuming Leadership: Community Colleges, Curriculum Reform and Teaching." *Educational Record,* 1994, 75 (1), 32–35.

Doucette, D. *Community College Workforce Training Programs for Employees of Business, Industry, Labor, and Government.* Los Angeles: League for Innovation in the Community College, 1993.

Eurich, N. P. *Corporate Classrooms: The Learning Business.* A Carnegie Foundation Special Report. Princeton, N.J.: Princeton University Press, Carnegie Foundation for the Advancement of Teaching, 1985.

Hagerstown Business College. *1992–1994 College Catalog.* Hagerstown, Md.: Hagerstown Business College, 1991.

Harris, J., Hillenmeyer, S., and Foran J. V. *Quality Assurance for Private Career Schools.* Washington, D.C.: AICS, McGraw-Hill 1989.

Hull, D. *Opening Minds, Opening Doors: The Rebirth of American Education.* Waco, Tex.: CORD Communications, 1993.

Jewel, R. "Interview." *Muskegon Chronicle,* Aug. 10, 1993.

Johnstone, D. "College at Work: The New Imperative for American Higher Education." *Educational Record,* 1993, *74* (1), 49–52.

Lorenzo, A. L., and Armes-LeCroy, N. "A Framework for Fundamental Change in the Community College." *Community College Journal,* 1994, *64* (4), 14–19.

Maryland State Department of Education, Division of Career, Technology, and Adult Learning. "Washington County Tech Prep Consortium Supplemental Grant," 1993–94.

Morris, W. V. "Avoiding Community Colleges: Students Who Attend Proprietary Vocational Schools." *Community College Journal of Research and Practice,* 1993, *17* (1), 21–28.

Reich, R. B. "Strategies for a Changing Workforce." *Educational Record,* 1993, *74* (4), 21–23.

Roueche, J. E., and Roueche, S. D. "Building Better Mousetraps and Tooting Horns: A Modest Proposal for Disseminating Teaching/Learning Innovation in the '90s." *Community College Journal,* 1994, *64* (5), 36–43.

Shaw, R. G. "Curriculum Change in the Community College: Pendulum Swing or Spiral Soar?" In T. O'Banion (ed.), *Innovation in the Community College.* New York: Macmillan, 1989.

Stadtman, V. A. (ed.). *Missions of the College Curriculum: A Contemporary Review with Suggestions.* San Francisco: Jossey-Bass, 1977.

Thompson, H. L. "New Relationships Between Universities, Community Colleges, and Technical Colleges." *Journal of Staff, Program, and Organization Development,* 1994, *11* (3).

Weingartner, R. H. "Between Cup and Lip: Reconceptualizing Education as Students Learn." *Educational Record,* 1994, *75* (1), 13–19.

Young, J. H. "Laying Stone on Sacred Stone: An Educational Foundation for the Future." *Educational Record,* 1994, *75* (1), 6–12.

CHERYL HYSLOP was dean of Hagerstown Business College and is currently executive director at Intellivoice Communications, Inc., Farmington Hills, Michigan.

MICHAEL H. PARSONS is dean of instruction at Hagerstown Junior College, Hagerstown, Maryland.

It appears that community college and proprietary school students differed more in the past than they do now; proprietary not-for-profit institutions may contribute to the apparent convergence.

Who Are the Students at Community Colleges and Proprietary Schools?

Xing David Cheng, Bernard H. Levin

Researchers remain divided regarding the basic demographic characteristics—gender, race, and socioeconomic status (SES)—of the proprietary school student. While a significant volume of research on proprietary students has been published during the past quarter century, we detect no movement toward consensus. Several factors may be operating, including differences in vintage; accidental and institution-based subject samples (for example, Wilms, 1974, 1980) versus national and stratified random samples (for example, Levin and Clowes, 1987); extreme variations in statistical treatment; and the issues concerning the definition of terms that are referred to above and in the text that follows. The result is a confusing, not very pretty picture.

In some literature, proprietary students are reported as disproportionally female (Levin and Clowes, 1987; Friedlander, 1980; Kincaid and Podesta, 1967). Other literature shows them to be male (Belitsky, 1969; Braden and Paul, 1971). In general, those researchers who agglomerate institution types or who focus on programs such as hair styling, health professions, data processing, and business report a predominantly female student population. Those researchers who focus on barbering, mechanical trades, truck driving, and (occasionally) business schools (for example, Hoyt, 1966–67) report predominantly male populations. The interaction of gender with curriculum is typical (Apling, 1993). Lee and Merisotis (1990) were correct when they claimed, "The tremendous variation in the types of programs offered at proprietary schools makes generalizations tenuous at best" (p. 19).

Extensive data tables supplementing the text are available in Cheng and Levin (1995).

NEW DIRECTIONS FOR COMMUNITY COLLEGES, no. 91, Fall 1995   © Jossey-Bass Publishers

Race may also interact with program type (Wolman, Campbell, Jung, and Richards, 1972). Three studies report that approximately 25 percent of their student population was black (Friedlander, 1980; Proprietary Education in Georgia, 1975; Doherty, 1973). The National Postsecondary Student Aid Study (1987) reports that 21 percent of proprietary students are African American, while 14 percent are Hispanic. Wolman, Campbell, Jung, and Richards (1972) claim that minorities would avoid proprietaries on cost grounds, while Wilms (1980) appears to claim that Hispanic and Asian minorities are disproportionally represented in proprietary institutions. While Levin and Clowes (1987) found that proprietary students are disproportionally likely to be white, and Apling (1993) found that proprietary students are disproportionally likely to be minorities, Wagner (1982) found that proprietary students and community college-technical institute students do not differ in race. Morris (1993) found that most of the subjects in his proprietary sample were black or Hispanic. Some care is urged in interpreting these differences. For example, Wilms used only four sites, two of which were in communities with a large Hispanic population. Further, Morris used only three sites; all were located in Hispanic areas.

The literature on the SES of proprietary students is also contradictory. The typical proprietary student has been reported to be from a middle-class family (Levin and Clowes, 1987), or from a blue-collar family (Juhlin, 1976; Morris, 1993), or from a family with below-average income (Apling, 1993; Morris, 1993), or from a lower-income family than the typical community college student (Apling, 1993; Friedlander, 1980; Christian, 1975; Wagner, 1982). The National Postsecondary Student Aid Study (1987) reports an average annual income below $11,000 but throws a new wrinkle into the data—this figure includes both dependent and independent students. Juhlin (1976) does report an anomaly—white proprietary students are disproportionally from high-income families. Finally, in three articles over three years, Wilms himself found conflicting results (1973, 1974, 1975).

Researchers tend to agree that most proprietary students are from less-educated families, at least less educated than those attending community colleges and four-year institutions. Morris (1993) maintains that the parental background of proprietary students is "predominantly uneducated" (p. 25). For 20 percent of proprietary students, neither parent had graduated high school (Apling, 1993). Proprietary students also may be less independent. Korb (1988) reports that about half of proprietary students (and college students) live with their parents. Morris (1993) reports that "Despite a mean age of more than 26, 4 out of 5 subjects were . . . still living with their parents" (p. 25).

It is also commonly believed that proprietary students' academic background is weaker than those attending community colleges and four-year institutions. The National Postsecondary Student Aid Study (1987) reports that the academic ability of proprietary students is lower than that of college students. Nonetheless, Levin and Clowes (1987) found a composite aptitude score to be unrelated to selection of a proprietary or not-for-profit institution as opposed to a two-year institution. Using a self-report measure, Morris's (1993) proprietary students had a high school mean grade point average of slightly less than 3.0. Friedlander's (1980) conclusion is nearly identical.

There are some gray areas in the literature concerning proprietary students' academic credentials. One report, "Proprietary Education in Georgia" (1975), indicates up to 10 percent of proprietary students already have at least a two-year degree. Hanson and Parker (1977) emphasize that most proprietary school students are high school dropouts, and some reports state that most proprietary school students have a high school diploma (Friedlander, 1980; Juhlin, 1976; Morris, 1993). Levin and Clowes (1987) and the National Postsecondary Student Aid Study (1987) found that proprietary students are likely to have been in a vocational-technical program in high school. In addition, students' transfer activities to and from proprietaries certainly add to the complexity of this issue of credentials.

Moore and Kuchinke's (1991) study on private career schools shows that, in Minnesota, fully one-third of the proprietary students had tried a community college before attending a proprietary school. In a statewide survey of Virginia private career schools, Moore and Smith (1991) found that nearly half of all proprietary students had attended another institution. Among those who had attended another institution, about half had attended a community college and over one-third had attended a four-year institution.

Finally, numerous studies have assessed the educational attainment of students at two- and four-year colleges and universities. However, very little has been done to measure proprietary student educational attainment, nor has much been said about proprietary students' aspirations and dreams for higher education. Morris (1993) says that "more than three fourths of the interview sample anticipated completing at least an associate's degree at some later time" (p. 26). But he also reinforces the suspicion of many researchers and counselors that educational aspirations may lack a reality check—26 percent of his proprietary sample anticipated earning a master's degree or doctorate. Cheng, Clowes, and Muffo (1992) found that the educational attainment of proprietary students was significantly lower than that of community college students, and community college students' attainment was lower than that of four-year students.

Method

Findings reported in this study are based on an extract file from High School and Beyond (HSB), a nationwide longitudinal study of high school students sponsored by the National Center for Education Statistics (NCES) of the U.S. Department of Education. The data include the base-year survey, which was conducted in 1980, and three follow-up surveys through 1986. The senior cohort data were used in this study, and that sample includes a total of 11,995 students.

An NCES-generated program was used to identify respondents' patterns of attendance in different types of postsecondary institutions. For those who attended more than one school from 1980 to 1986, the first postsecondary institution was used to place the student into one of four types of institutional attendance for purposes of this study. These four types of postsecondary institutions are (1) proprietary schools (PROP); (2) private, not-for-profit schools (NFP), including both two-year and less-than-two-year institutions; (3) two-year public institutions (2YR), mostly community colleges, but also including some less-than-two-year schools; and (4) four-year institutions (4YR), including both public and private colleges and universities.

Since respondents' patterns of postsecondary enrollment are based on self-reported variables, we suspect that at least two factors might contribute to the relatively small sample size for PROPs and NFPs as compared to 2YR and 4YR samples. First, some PROP and NFP programs are so short that respondents did not even count them as part of their postsecondary experience. Second, PROP and NFP schools are not the first choices for most high school graduates, at least not for the first few years after high school graduation. While crossing the PROP and NFP samples with other variables, we suffered further loss of data due to missing cases in one or more variables. We chose not to make any estimation to make up these losses for fear of disturbing the result.

Another limitation of the HSB senior data is that those who dropped out of school prior to the twelfth grade are not included at all. We are not aware of any research on proprietary students that examines separately those who dropped out prior to twelfth grade. Thus, we have no basis for guessing whether our results and conclusions might have been different had the dropouts been included. The remainder of this text should be viewed with these limitations in mind.

Results

Both PROPs and NFPs are twice as likely to be female as male. In contrast, both 2YRs and 4YRs are only 54 percent female. Also, blacks are nearly three times as likely to attend PROPs as NFPs, but more than 57 percent of blacks in postsecondary institutions are in 4YRs. A similar pattern holds for whites in that whites are more than twice as likely to attend a PROP as an NFP, but 58 percent of whites in postsecondary institutions are in a 4YR institution. The pattern of Hispanic attendance is quite different. Hispanics are about fifty times as likely to attend a 2YR school and six times as likely to attend a PROP, compared to an NFP. More than half of Hispanics in postsecondary institutions are in 2YR institutions.

As one ascends SES, the likelihood of attending a 4YR increases and the likelihood of the other three alternatives decreases. Not surprisingly, family income shows a pattern similar to SES. The higher the income, the less likely is attendance at a PROP or NFP or 2YR. Parental education evinces the same sort of relationship as SES and family income. The higher the educational level of the parent, the less likely the student is to attend either a PROP or an NFP or a 2YR.

For example, of students whose parents had earned no more than a high school diploma, 7.9 percent attended a PROP. In contrast, of students whose parents had earned at least a masters degree, only 1.9 percent attended a PROP.

Dependency or immaturity does not seem to characterize PROP and NFP students. Those who attended 4YR institutions are the least-independent group, while NFP students turned out to be the most independent. In general, from one-half to two-thirds of postsecondary students either still lived with their parents or other guardians or did not have their own home, apartment, or other residence six years after their high school graduation.

A series of cognitive tests was administered to HSB participants in order to measure their verbal and quantitative abilities. The general belief was confirmed that the higher the test quartile, the less likely the student is to attend either a PROP or an NFP or a 2YR. The distribution pattern of the four quartile groups is very similar between NFPs and 2YRs. The striking contrast exists between PROPs and 4YRs: almost five times as many first-quartile students as fourth-quartile students attended PROPs, while more than three times as many fourth-quartile students as first-quartile students attended 4YR institutions.

Although some of the samples are small, it is clear that the pattern of high school grades for the noncollegiate institutions is much different from the four-year patterns. Among PROP, NFP, and 2YR students, the median grade in high school was B. In contrast, the median grade in high school for 4YR students was A.

PROP's appeal to students from different types of high schools is similar to that of 2YRs. On the other hand, 4YRs attracted disproportionally more private and Catholic high school graduates. Students from urban high schools are more likely than rural or suburban students to attend PROPs. Urban students are less likely to attend NFPs. Neither 2YR nor 4YR attendance seems much affected by locus of high school.

Two-thirds of 4YR students had been in an academic program while in high school. In contrast, only 20 percent of PROP students, 31 percent of two-year students, and 41 percent of NFP students had been in an academic high school program. The present data show that almost all PROP students are high school graduates. The proportion of high school dropouts in PROPs and NFPs is only trivially different from that in 2YR and 4YR institutions.

Another way to look at PROP and NFP students' academic ability is to see if these students have any postsecondary experience before and after their study in a noncollegiate school. Our data show that about one-third of PROP and NFP students transferred to a 2YR or 4YR institution, and about one-third of 2YR students transferred to 4YR institutions. Reverse transfer is common. Between 5 and 6 percent of 2YR and 4YR students transferred to PROP and NFP schools. Over one-fifth of 4YR students transferred to 2YR institutions. Further, the number of students transferring from 2YR to 4YR is not much different from the number of students transferring from 4YR to 2YR.

A comparison between students' educational aspirations and their attainment reveals interesting results. A first glance at the data shows that PROP students are the ones with the lowest educational aspirations: 16 percent of them never had any postsecondary education aspirations or plans versus only 2 percent of 4YR students; the proportion of PROP students aspiring to a four-year degree is also significantly lower than that of other students. However, PROPs seem to be very effective in bringing vocational and technical education to those who aspired to something other than traditional baccalaureate degrees or higher. While 61 percent of PROP students aspired to (and over one-half of them received) a license, certificate, or two-year vocational degree, fewer than one-half of 2YR students had the same aspirations, and fewer than one-third of them actually reached their goals six years after high school graduation. Not surprisingly, while 23 percent of PROP students aspired to a four-year degree or higher, only 0.7 percent of them reached their goal. However, if we look at the overall educational attainment at different levels, it is clear that NFP students display a pattern very similar to their 2YR counterparts: while 38 percent of NFP students completed a vocational program or degree and 8.7 percent received a four-year degree, 32 percent and 7.8 percent respectively in 2YRs did so.

Discussion

Our results indicate that the often controversial depictions of student demographic characteristics at proprietary schools reflect to a certain extent the complex student body in these schools. However, while comparing the so-called proprietaries (including PROPs and NFPs) and community colleges, the trend of convergence is apparent. For instance, about 60 percent of students at both PROPs and 2YRs were minorities; also, the lower a student's SES, family income level, and parental education level, the more likely that student is to attend a PROP, an NFP, or a 2YR. With respect to academic background, 4YR students were clearly stronger than their counterparts in other types of schools. This relatively disadvantageous position for PROP, NFP, and 2YR students in academic background is further evident when the variables of high school type, high school program, and educational attainment come into play: the proportion of students from private high schools in four-year institutions is much higher than that in the other three types of postsecondary institutions; two-thirds of students in four-year institutions are from an academic high school program, while the other three types of institution have from one-fifth to two-fifths academic high school students; and finally, while nearly two-fifths of students attending four-year institutions received at least a bachelor's degree in a six-year period, less than one-tenth in each of the other three types achieved the same.

The HSB data allow us to look into the two major sectors within the proprietaries—private, for-profit and private, not-for-profit—and reveal some previously unknown commonalities and differences between the schools generally called "proprietaries" and community colleges.

First, the ethnic composition of PROPs and NFPs for these two groups of schools differs to a certain extent. While approximately 60 percent of students in PROPs and 2YRs are minorities, a majority of students attending NFPs and 4YRs are white. Apparently, in terms of serving minority groups, NFP schools display a pattern similar to four-year institutions. This may be one of the reasons researchers differ in estimating ethnic composition in different types of institutions when PROPs and NFPs are combined. Otherwise, ethnic composition in different types of postsecondary institutions remains complicated. Blacks and whites are equally likely to attend 4YRs (57 and 58 percent, respectively), while considerably fewer (41 percent) Hispanics attend 4YRs. More than half of Hispanics choose 2YRs as their postsecondary option, in contrast with only one-third of blacks and whites. Neither PROPs nor NFPs account for as much as 8 percent of any racial or ethnic group. These attendance patterns require further study.

Second, NFP students' relatively high-SES family background seems to have brought a combined PROP and NFP group level closer to that for community colleges. For instance, NFPs served more high-SES students than PROPs (42 percent versus 31 percent). NFPs attracted more middle-class (with family income between $20,000 and $37,000) background students than PROPs and even slightly more than 2YRs. Also, 11 percent of NFP students' parents have a college degree or higher, as compared to fewer than 7 percent for PROPs.

Third, NFP students' aptitude test scores are also higher than that of PROPs. NFPs display a pattern similar to 2YRs with respect to students' academic background. Compared to 2YRs, NFPs actually attracted slightly more students in the third test quartile and with mostly A grades in high school. What is even more surprising is that the likelihood of an NFP student coming from an academic high school program is two times higher than that of a PROP student and one-quarter higher than a 2YR college student. As a result, the proportion of NFP students who eventually received a baccalaureate degree is also closer to or even slightly higher than that of 2YR students. These findings indicate that NFP students are less "disadvantaged" academically and that they have a higher potential for educational attainment, compared to other proprietary students.

Another difficult issue is how to compare the outcomes and effectiveness of proprietaries and community colleges. Each school is set up to implement its own mission. The common wisdom is that proprietaries were always leaning toward utilitarian purposes, while community colleges were more for general lower-division education. Our study of proprietary students' transfer behavior reveals the possibility that proprietary and especially NFP students in the long run may not be so desperate for "quick, specialized training to gain employment" (Morris, 1993) as they appear to be on matriculation. In fact, one-third of these students transferred to a 2YR or 4YR institution in a six-year period. This at least shows that they aspire to attain higher levels of postsecondary education. When we compare the educational attainment of PROP and NFP students with those in 2YRs, we find that 60 percent of 2YR students had not received anything more than a high school diploma six years after high school, but the comparable figure for PROP students is only 48 percent. Meanwhile, over one-half of PROP students received a license, certificate, or associate degree in a six-year period, as compared to fewer than one-third of 2YR students. Then why have so few PROP students moved further to successfully receive a baccalaureate degree compared to their NFP and 2YR counterparts? Our data support the assertion by Cheng, Clowes, and Muffo (1992) that the low aptitude and relatively poor academic background of these students hinder their achievement in higher education.

Since the major mission for most PROP and NFP schools is vocational education and job training, our data lead to the conclusion that these schools have done reasonably well in meeting the students' needs. The vocational orientation of PROP and NFP programs appeals to those who neither aspire to nor possess the skills sufficient to earn an academic degree, though the preceding is more true of PROP than of NFP. Proprietary schools have helped raise the educational levels of a great number of young adults to a considerable height, given the relatively low aptitude and low SES of their students. This is another area where proprietaries and community colleges come close to each other.

We conclude that proprietaries and community colleges have not been serving the same students in the past (Levin and Clowes, 1987), though the type of students each is serving has changed a bit. A factor that needs to be taken into account is the private not-for-profit sector. Their students certainly do not fit the overall picture of proprietary students. Whether the characteristics of proprietary students will eventually move closer to those of community college students is speculative. However, if community colleges begin to emphasize noncredit training as a major center for growth and profit (Levin and Perkins, in press), we expect that convergence in student bodies will follow this convergence in mission.

We consider the separate treatment of NFPs a very important factor in any future studies on proprietary schools. On a practical level, we recommend that market researchers carefully examine the strategies used by proprietaries and community colleges, including their effectiveness and efficiency as related to mission. Such examination not only would benefit the daily operations of both types of institutions but also would have the potential to improve their strategic planning and policy-making processes.

References

Apling, R. N. "Proprietary Schools and Their Students." *Journal of Higher Education,* 1993, 64 (4), 379–416.

Belitsky, A. H. *Private Vocational Schools and Their Students: Limited Objectives, Unlimited Opportunities.* Cambridge, Mass.: Shenkman, 1969.

Braden, P. V., and Paul, K. K. "Vocational Education and Private Schools." In G. F. Law (ed.), *Contemporary Concepts in Vocational Education.* Washington D.C.: American Vocational Association, 1971, 200–204.

Cheng, X., Clowes, D. A., and Muffo, J. A. "Assessing the Educational Attainment of Proprietary Students from National Data." Unpublished report, 1992. (ED 342 458)

Cheng, X. D., and Levin, B. H. "Demographic Characteristics, Academic Background, and Educational Aspirations of Community College and Proprietary School Students." Unpublished report, 1995. (ERIC data base document; ED number not yet assigned.)

Christian, C. E. "Analysis of a Pilot Survey of Proprietary Schools." Los Angeles: Higher Education Research Institute, 1975.

Doherty, G. P. "Case Study: The Bell and Howell Schools." In D. W. Vermilye (ed.), *The Future in the Making*. San Francisco: Jossey-Bass, 1973.

Friedlander, M. C. *Characteristics of Students Attending Proprietary Schools and Factors Influencing Their Institutional Choice*. Cincinnati, Ohio: South-Western, 1980.

Hanson, G. A., and Parker, E. C. "The Vocational Education Industry." In W. G. Meyer (ed.), *Vocational Education and the Nation's Economy*. Washington, D.C.: American Vocational Association, 1977.

Hoyt, K. B. "The Vanishing American." *Delta Pi Epsilon Journal,* 1966–67, *9* (2), 1–8.

Juhlin, L. A. *Characteristics of Students Enrolled in Resident Proprietary Schools in Illinois*. Carbondale: Southern Illinois University, 1976.

Kincaid, H. V., and Podesta, E. A. "An Exploratory Socio-Economic Study of Private Vocational Schools," 1967.

Korb, R., Schantz, N., Stowe, P., and Zimbler, L. "Undergraduate Financing of Postsecondary Education: A Report of the 1987 National Postsecondary Student Aid Study." Washington, D.C.: U.S. Department of Education, Office of Educational Research and Improvement, National Center for Education Statistics, 1988.

Lee, J. B., and Merisotis, J. P. *Proprietary Schools: Programs, Policies, and Prospects*. ASHE-ERIC Higher Education Report No. 5. Washington, D.C.: School of Education and Human Development, George Washington University, 1990. (ED 331 337)

Levin, B. H., and Clowes, D. A. "Competition Between Community Colleges and Postsecondary Proprietary Schools: Reality or Myth?" *Journal of Studies in Technical Careers,* 1987, *9* (4), 317–323.

Levin, B. H., and Perkins, J. R. "The Future of Community College Continuing Education." *Catalyst,* in press.

Moore, R. W., and Kuchinke, K. P. "The Role and Quality of Proprietary Schools: Minnesota Students' Perspective." Paper presented at the annual convention of the American Educational Research Association, Chicago, 1991.

Moore, R. W., and Smith, E. J. "Student Perspective on Quality: A Quality Assessment of Virginia Private Career Schools." Research report sponsored by the Virginia Association on Private Career Schools, 1991.

Morris, W. V. "Avoiding Community Colleges: Students Who Attend Proprietary Vocational Schools." *Community College Journal of Research and Practice,* 1993, *17* (1), 21–28.

National Postsecondary Student Aid Study. Washington, D.C.: U.S. Department of Education, Office of Educational Research and Improvement, National Center for Education Statistics, 1987.

"Proprietary Education in Georgia." Atlanta: Georgia State Postsecondary Education Commission, 1975. (ED 138 746)

Wagner, A. P. "Postcompulsory Education and Training: An Inventory of Programs and Sources of Support." *Education and Urban Society,* 1982, *14,* 271–300.

Wilms, W. W. *Proprietary Versus Public Vocational Education*. Berkeley: Center for Research and Development in Higher Education, University of California, 1973.

Wilms, W. W. "Proprietary and Public Vocational Students." *Collegiate and University Bulletin,* 1974, *26* (7), 3–6.

Wilms, W. W. *Public and Proprietary Vocational Training: A Study of Effectiveness*. Lexington, Mass.: D.C. Heath, 1975.

Wilms, W. W. "Vocational Education and Social Mobility: A Study of Public and Proprietary School Dropouts and Graduates." Los Angeles: Graduate School of Education, University of California, Los Angeles, 1980. (ED 183 966)

Wolman, J. M., Campbell, V. N., Jung, S. M., and Richards, J. M. *A Comparative Study of Proprietary and Non-Proprietary Vocational Training Programs.* Palo Alto, Calif.: American Institutes for Research in the Behavioral Sciences, 1972. (ED 067 523)

XING DAVID CHENG is coordinator of institutional research at Colorado Community College in Denver.

BERNARD H. LEVIN is professor of psychology at Blue Ridge Community College in Weyers Cave, Virginia.

The author shows default, accreditation, and articulation to be power-ful external factors that operate to force proprietary schools to become more like community colleges.

Ties That Bind: Default, Accreditation, and Articulation

Carolyn Prager

Like community colleges, private career schools have a hierarchical rather than a structural connection to higher education. For community colleges, this con-nection depends largely on a single phenomenon—the necessity of student transfer to a senior college to earn a bachelor's degree. Currently, the ties that bind community to senior colleges derive mostly from transfer. Colleges and universities, including community colleges, that fail to award credit for work successfully completed at accredited degree-granting proprietary schools deny them even this tenuous link to higher education. In addition to wasting pub-lic funds already invested in student financial assistance and depleting the human capital of students forced to repeat work unnecessarily, the failure to engage in meaningful transfer and articulation relationships with accredited proprietary schools undermines institutional self-interest in preserving volun-tary accreditation as a mark of acceptability for all colleges and universities, regardless of their corporate status.

In this chapter, I will examine the changed accreditation environment and the resulting implications for the articulation of for-profit to not-for-profit insti-tutions like community colleges. In doing so, I will also question the validity of continuing institutional policies at some public and private colleges and uni-versities that automatically invalidate the transfer of credit for work completed at proprietary institutions on the basis of different accrediting relationships.

Accreditation's Legitimacy

In the absence of a national centralized authority for education, accreditation arose in the United States to ensure a basic level of quality through nongovernmental, voluntary peer evaluation of educational institutions and programs. Regional and national private accreditation associations have adopted principles and procedures for evaluating institutions or programs to ascertain minimal standards of quality, honest practice, and realization of objectives.

There are two basic types of accreditation—institutional and specialized (programmatic). Specialized accreditation usually applies to particular institutional components such as programs, departments, or schools. Typically but not universally, specialized or programmatic accreditors review these institutional components within institutions of higher education already accredited by a regional commission. Some specialized or programmatic accrediting bodies may also accredit single-purpose, stand-alone institutions of higher education and, in that capacity, function as an institutional accrediting agency. In general, however, colleges and universities, including those referred to as private career schools, are accredited at the institutional level by regional or national accreditation associations. Historically, not-for-profit, degree-granting schools have acquired regional accreditation, while for-profit, degree-granting schools have tended to acquire national or, less frequently, both regional and national accreditation (Nash and Hawthorne, 1987).

By statute, the U.S. Secretary of Education must recognize (approve) accreditation agencies to ensure that these agencies are "for the purposes of the Higher Education Act of 1965, as amended (HEA), or for other Federal purposes, reliable authorities as to the quality of education or training offered by the institutions of higher education or the higher education programs they accredit" (Department of Education, 34 CFR Part 602, Subpart A, 602.1, 1994). In this context, accreditation legitimates higher education institutions. However, it does not guarantee automatic acceptance by one institution of credit earned at another, even among institutions certified by the same regional accreditor, let alone among degree-granting schools certified by different institutional accreditors.

The amendments to the HEA of 1992 focused primarily on monitoring default. However, the legislation also actually encourages institutions and their external evaluators to move beyond default and assess quality by including outcome measures such as program completion rates, student attainment of occupational competency, and labor market performance.

In principle, colleges and universities prize accreditation as a measure of respectability. Nonetheless, in practice they may accept transfer credit from some accredited institutions but not from others, particularly proprietary ones without regional accreditation. This practice contravenes the spirit and text of the *Joint Statement on Transfer and Award of Academic Credit* approved by the Council on Postsecondary Accreditation, the American Council of Education, and the American Association of Collegiate Registrars and Admissions Officers in 1978 and the American Association of Community and Junior Colleges (AACJC) in 1990, which stipulates that "transfer of credit is a concept that *now* [emphasis added] involves transfer between dissimilar institutions and curricula . . . as well as . . . [those] of similar characteristics" (American Association of Community and Junior Colleges, 1992, p. 183). The *Joint Statement* encourages colleges and universities to have confidence in the recognition of educational quality implied in accreditation, including accreditation by national accrediting bodies, since "all accrediting bodies that meet COPA's standards for recognition function to assure that the institutions or programs have met generally accepted minimum standards for accreditation" (p. 183).

Accredited Private Career Colleges

Of necessity, private career schools have responded substantively to more stringent accreditation standards brought about by public pressure for accountability due to student loan default. As they have done so, they have increased their potential for conversion to private career colleges and universities by offering degrees in programs often found in public, two-year institutions. From a public policy perspective, this can either increase the danger of needless competition and duplication or enhance the opportunities for cooperation and coordination.

The Florida State University State and Regional Higher Education Center found 231 associate degree-granting institutions with Internal Revenue Service-designated proprietary status for 1989, sixty-two of them accredited by regional associations (Bender, 1991). Replicating the Center's methodology for 1992, I identified 277 accredited associate degree-granting institutions, twenty-seven of them regionally accredited. Seventy-six offered an associate degree that is creditable toward a baccalaureate in programs designed specifically for transfer. I did not list branches as separately accredited entities, and the Florida study may have. This may account for some or all of the apparent sharp decline in the number of regionally accredited two-year schools noted in the two studies. Or, the decline may have been a real one marked by increasing reliance on national as opposed to regional accreditation by the private career colleges.

Based on these figures, the total number of two-year, degree-awarding private career colleges appears to have grown more than 16 percent in this three-year period. More appear to have followed the national accreditation path than ever before, either through the renamed Accrediting Commission of Career Schools and Colleges of Technology (the former National Association of Trade and Technical Schools) or the Accrediting Commission for Independent Colleges and Schools.

Proprietary Accountability Through Accreditation

In recent years, we have witnessed a remarkable change in both the degree and the kind of accreditation activity affecting proprietary institutions. In academic year 1988–89, there were an estimated 6,200 schools (including branch campuses) constituting over one-half of the nation's postsecondary institutions. About 6 percent offered associate degrees. In the mid 1980s, non–correspondence schools enrolled between 1.2 and 1.6 million students

(Apling, 1993). Because of Title IV eligibility requirements, the number of *accredited* proprietary schools appears to have increased dramatically since the mid 1970s, even though the total number of proprietary schools appears to have declined (Apling, 1993).

In 1987, the Carnegie Foundation for the Advancement of Teaching noted that the percentage of career schools accredited by national agencies had grown from about one-third in 1978 to a little less than one-half in 1982. In 1990, the General Accounting Office (GAO) presented a briefing report to a Senate subcommittee listing seven national and one regional agency that had accredited 5,585 proprietaries and their branches from fiscal year 1985 through fiscal year 1989. In another study, proprietary school associations reported 5,992 accreditations by national *or* regional associations among their approximately 4,000 schools and 2,000 campuses for 1989 (Apling, 1993). Since these studies may or may not have distinguished between separately accredited schools and branch campuses and may have included duplicated counts from institutions with more than one accreditation, the data can only attest to an increase in accreditation activity in both degree and in kind.

Although most private career colleges now pursue the national accreditation route, some still participate in regional accreditation. Accreditation by a single regional accreditor—the Southern Association of Colleges and Schools, Commission on Occupational Education Institutions, for example—accounted for almost 14 percent of the 5,992 accreditations cited above for 1989.

Regional Accreditation of Private Career Schools

Undoubtedly, tensions may exist within the regional associations arising from lack of familiarity with the proprietary culture (Young, 1987). Nonetheless, regional accreditors appear to evaluate private career schools according to the same criteria and in the same fashion as other postsecondary institutions, with due allowances for contextual differences.

The regional associations vary in their organizational structure. This means that the Middle States Association, the North Central Association, the Southern Association, and the Northwest Association accredit proprietary institutions like all other degree-granting institutions and use the same commissions, or both. However, the New England Association of Schools and Colleges reviews proprietary schools in the same commission as other public or private "specialized institutions of higher education," awarding an associate degree at the technical or career level through its Commission on Vocational, Technical, and Career Institutions, while the Western Association accredits public, private, independent, and proprietary two-year, degree-granting schools through its Commission for Community and Junior Colleges.

Middle States Association of Colleges and Schools. The Middle States Association does not differentiate between eligible private career schools and other colleges and universities in its accreditation guidelines. It does set forth a basic set of considerations for evaluators visiting proprietary postsecondary degree-granting institutions who may be less familiar with the for-profit educational environment (Middle States Association of Colleges and Schools, 1984). Through a series of guiding questions, the document encourages evaluators to look for evidence of state and specialized programmatic approvals, of sound management practices related to instructional matters, of sound fiscal management, of faculty load and distribution, of library holdings, and of other elements arising from contextual differences associated with for-profit schools.

Western Association of Schools and Colleges. The Western Association's *Handbook of Accreditation and Policy Manual* (1990) embraces "the community of community, junior, and specialized two year colleges" (introduction). The *Handbook* contains a separate full-page statement addressed specifically to "general education in specialized programs and institutions" (p. 48), which signals the attention the Association gives to general education in such institutions. It also contains language stressing the need for formal processes providing for faculty participation in institutional governance (Standard 8D.1, p. 39).

New England Association of Schools and Colleges. Unlike the other regional accreditors, the New England Association has enunciated separate *Standards of Membership* for "specialized institutions of higher education awarding an associate degree at the technical or career level" (New England Association of Schools and Colleges, 1993) that address specifically the environmentally contextual differences. These include special attention to governance, finance, faculty, and general education. For example, their *Standards* call for clearly defined faculty involvement in the formulation of educational policy, evidence of sound financial structure, a substantial majority of faculty teaching full-time, and at least twenty hours of general education.

National Institutional Accreditation of Private Career Schools

The national institutional accreditors of degree-granting private career schools now hold the campuses they evaluate to qualitative standards that equal and, in some cases, exceed those promulgated by the regional commissions. However, some critics point to pressures that could compromise the accreditors' capacity to enforce standards (Fitzgerald and Harmon, 1988). These include the huge numbers of institutions seeking membership in one or more of the national accrediting groups, the difficulty in monitoring branching, and the competition for membership possibly compromising the accreditors' capacity to enforce standards (Fitzgerald and Harmon, 1988). In the most comprehensive study of proprietary schools to date, Lee and Merisotis (1990) state that the "pivotal policy question . . . is whether the standards established by the organizations [i.e., the accreditors] are sufficient" (p. 69) for proprietary institutions. That is, of course, a critical question but one that should be applied to the entire accreditation universe, not only to the national accreditors of for-profit colleges.

National accrediting association practices are observable but remain largely unstudied in a sustained scholarly fashion, like most other areas related to proprietary school activity. Both recruit at least one person not representative of an institution they accredit for private career college visiting teams, including representation from community colleges, when appropriate. Based on the available evidence, however, it is clear that the national associations accrediting private career colleges have tightened their standards and review procedures considerably in recent years. Between fiscal years 1985 and 1989, the National Association of Trade and Technical Schools (NATTS) accredited 641 schools, initially deferred 157, denied 70, and terminated the reaccreditation of 69; the AICS accredited 149, initially deferred 0, denied 120, and terminated 55 (GAO, 1990). In 1988 alone, NATTS denied 11 percent of those seeking accreditation and 5 percent of those seeking reaccreditation (Carson, 1989).

Qualitative National Association Accreditation Standards. The national associations accrediting private career schools have responded substantively to public pressure for accountability generated in large measure by the default issue by establishing more stringent requirements for accreditation called for by the amendments to the HEA of 1992. The Accrediting Commission of Career Schools and Colleges of Technology (ACCSCT) and the Accrediting Commission of the Association of Independent Colleges and Schools (ACAICS) have promulgated standards in recent years that address those qualitative factors often cited as persistent weaknesses—faculty preparation and academic participation, institutional financial stability, student services provision, and separate branch campus regulation. The accrediting policies enunciated by these national associations have implications for credit transfer from for-profit to not-for-profit institutions and program articulation between them, to the extent that they establish clear academic priorities compatible with those of other collegiate institutions offering similar occupational and technical instruction.

Accrediting Commission of Career Schools and Colleges of Technology (ACCSCT). The introduction to the ACCSCT's *Standards of Accreditation* (1993) stresses the importance of outcome measures, including not only quantitative indices such as graduation rates, placement records, employer satisfaction, student satisfaction, and student success over time but also qualitative ones such as "specific skills, knowledge, and behaviors achieved by students as a direct result of participation in a training program" (p. 1). In other words, the ACCSCT makes explicit the evidentiary basis for determining outcomes within their *Standards*.

The ACCSCT sets standards for the occupational degree Associate in Occupational Studies and the "academic" (*Standards,* section IV.A., p. 11) degrees, the Associate of Arts, Associate of Science, or the Associate of Applied Arts and Science. The standards for these degrees stipulate that full-time faculty should teach the majority of instructional hours. ACCSCT standards require that technical course instructors have at least three years of practical work experience or equivalent training in the field being taught and that general education faculty hold a baccalaureate degree at the minimum. At first glance, the low baseline for faculty qualifications may appear to be a noticeable deficiency. However, the ACCSCT standards for faculty preparation depart little from prevailing ones set for occupational faculty by some specialized programmatic accreditors for career curricula offered at colleges and universities (Prager, 1992).

The associate degree requirement for fifteen semester hours of general education (*Standards,* section IV.C.1.c, p. 13) approximates the 25 percent recommended by the AACJC for the Associate in Applied Science degrees and parallels that required by the Southern Association for comparable collegiate programs. Other regional accreditors leave it to the institutions or to the states to set academic minimums for general education. The ACCSCT requires that students admitted to degree programs shall possess a high school diploma or recognized equivalency certificate (Section IV.C.2.a, p. 14). The "ability-to-benefit" (Section IV.C.2.b, p. 14) clause differs little from those articulated for not-for-profit institutions. Commission standards now speak directly to the social responsibilities the "ability-to-benefit" clause entails. The standards require an appropriate student services program including, at a minimum, academic advising and personal counseling, attendance monitoring, placement assistance, and information services related to housing, transportation, child care, and relevant coping skills (Section VI.A.3, p. 15). Since August, 1990, the *Standards* have also contained stringent guidelines for the separate accreditation of branch facilities, and as of July, 1993, revised and stronger language regarding Commission approval of the transfer of accreditation upon change of ownership.

Accrediting Commission of the Association of Independent Colleges and Schools (ACAICS). The ACAICS *Criteria* (1991) states that the Association exists primarily to accredit three types of institutions that train people for business or business-related careers—business schools, which may award a diploma, a certificate, or a degree; junior colleges awarding a college degree; and senior colleges offering undergraduate and graduate degrees. "General Standards" applicable to all institutions call for each to demonstrate how it meets "its own predetermined outcomes" (Chapter 1, 3–1-110, p. 35). This is in keeping with the fundamental philosophical principles currently underlying accreditation, as espoused by both regional and national accreditation bodies. Within this theoretical framework, the ACAICS *Criteria* (1991) calls for evidence of student retention and placement to be evaluated according to institutionally stated goals. The document also calls for evidence of a collegial organizational structure that respects the professional integrity of faculty and staff, protects the faculty's academic freedom, and contributes to their professional growth (Section 3–1-200, 201, and 545, pp. 36, 37, and 50).

The *Criteria* states that faculty preparation need only be "academically and experientially appropriate to the subject matter that they teach" (Section 3–1-530, p. 50). However, full- and part-time faculty members teaching business, business administration, secretarial science, and related computer subjects must possess the baccalaureate at a minimum. Like the ACCSCT, the ACAICS mandates a minimum of fifteen semester hours of general education in associate degree programs. The ACAICS reminds its membership, however, that other external benchmarks exist in curriculum matters. It, therefore, requires that its member institutions "shall quantitatively and qualitatively approximate the standards at all other collegiate institutions offering associate degrees, with due allowance for meeting special objectives" (Section 3–3-203, p. 57).

Branch Campus Accreditation. Effective April 23, 1993, the ACAICS also adopted stringent language calling for an unannounced visit at each accredited site and a mandatory reinstatement accreditation visit within six months in the case of change of ownership or control. The toughened standards reflect Department of Education calls for compliance with the amendments to the HEA of 1992 criteria for definition of, site visits of, and business plans for branch campuses. The procedures related to branch campus accreditation specified in both the ACAICS and ACCSCT's current accreditation guidelines arose in response to perceived abuses in the unregulated expansion of proprietary branch campuses. Currently, they exceed those for branch campuses set by the regional accreditors on the whole in terms of focus, clarity, and expectations.

Accreditation, Transfer, and Articulation

Many public and private not-for-profit colleges and universities continue to reject the transfer of credit from private career colleges unless accredited by a regional accreditor, while most private career colleges continue to maintain institutional accreditation through a national rather than a regional association. "From a purely practical standpoint, the fact that private career education is inadequately articulated with traditional sector programs is a gigantic waste of both taxpayers' dollars and human capital" (Kimberling, 1987, p. 11). Proponents of increased articulation with proprietary schools argue this public policy perspective. Peterson (1982) goes so far as to suggest that public interest rather than market forces should dictate the level of interinstitutional, intersector cooperation.

The best available evidence, however, suggests that few students transfer from private career schools to other institutional types, a surprising phenomenon given the magnitude of the enrollment pool (Bergstrom and others, 1986; Bender, 1991) and the socioeconomic connection between education and career mobility. To what extent does the lack of articulation activity and the prospect of needless repetition of work successfully completed discourage their transfer? There is limited evidence of actual collaboration between proprietary institutions and other forms of postsecondary education, except for occasional instances at the local level (see, for example, Peterson, 1982; Lerner, 1987; Naylor, 1987; Robertson-Smith, 1990).

From a public policy perspective, national accreditation confers upon private career colleges the same acceptability in the new accreditation environment as that conferred by regional accreditation with the potential for improving the transfer and articulation climate. Conceivably, some regionally accredited institutions may demonstrate marginal quality and financial stability, while some nationally accredited ones may manifest the highest of standards. As Millard declares in *Today's Myths and Tomorrow's Realities*, it would be extraordinarily difficult to prove that "quality is a function of governance and ownership rather than of accomplishing educational objectives" (1991, p. 51). The cost of programmatic redundancy and duplication brought about by mission convergence at community colleges, proprietary institutions, and other postsecondary vocational providers is bound to emerge as a major public policy issue in the near future. At a minimum, the public has the right to expect that students who complete programs supported by public dollars in one educational format meeting comparable qualitative tests should be allowed to move on to another educational format without penalty to either the student or the taxpayer.

References

Accrediting Commission of Career Schools and Colleges of Technology. *Standards of Accreditation.* Washington, D.C.: Accrediting Commission of Career Schools and Colleges of Technology, 1993.

Accrediting Commission of the Association of Independent Colleges and Schools. *Accreditation Criteria: Policies, Procedures, and Standards.* Washington, D.C.: Accrediting Commission of the Association of Independent Colleges and Schools, 1991.

American Association of Community and Junior Colleges. "Policy Statement on the Associate of Applied Science Degree." In *AACJC Membership Directory 1992.* Washington, D.C.: American Association of Community and Junior Colleges, 1992.

Apling, R. N. "Proprietary Schools and Their Students." *Journal of Higher Education,* 1993, *64* (4), 379–416.

Bender, L. W. "Applied Associate Degree Transfer Phenomenon: Proprietaries and Publics." *Community College Review,* 1991, *19* (3), 22–28.

Bergstrom, D., and others. *Task Force on Private Proprietary Schools: Report to the Legislature.* St. Paul: Minnesota State Task Force on Private Proprietary Schools, Feb. 1986. (ED 289 030)

Carnegie Foundation for the Advancement of Teaching. "Career Schools: An Overview." *Change,* 1987, *19* (1), 29–34.

Carson, W. C. "Majority of Private Trade Schools Are a Success." *New York Times,* Mar. 29, 1989.

Department of Education. *Federal Register: Secretary's Procedures and Criteria for Recognition of Accrediting Agencies; Final Rule.* Washington, D.C.: Department of Education, Apr. 29, 1994.

Fitzgerald, B., and Harmon, L. *Consumer Rights and Accountability in Postsecondary Vocational-Technical Education: An Exploratory Study.* Washington, D.C.: Pelavin Associates, 1988.

General Accounting Office. *School Accreditation Activities of Seven Agencies That Accredit Proprietary Schools. Briefing Report to the Chairman, Permanent Subcommittee on Investigations, Committee on Governmental Affairs, U.S. Senate.* Washington, D.C.: General Accounting Office, 1990.

Kimberling, C. R. "Private Career Education: Opportunities and Challenges." *Career Training,* 1987, *4* (2), 10–11.

Lee, J. B., and Merisotis, J. P. *Proprietary Schools: Programs, Policies, and Prospects.* ASHE-ERIC Higher Education Report No. 5. Washington, D.C.: School of Education and Human Development, George Washington University, 1990. (ED 331 337)

Lerner, M. J. *Articulation Manual: A Guide for Transfer of Credit Between Educational Institutions.* Washington, D.C.: National Association of Trade and Technical Schools, 1987.

Middle States Association of Colleges and Schools, Commission on Higher Education.

"Evaluation of Proprietary Institutions for Accreditation." Philadelphia: Middle States Association of Colleges and Schools, 1984.

Millard, R. M. *Today's Myths and Tomorrow's Realities: Overcoming Obstacles to Academic Leadership in the 21st Century.* San Francisco: Jossey-Bass, 1991.

Nash, N. S., and Hawthorne, E. J. *Formal Recognition of Employer-Sponsored Instruction: Conflict and Collegiality in Postsecondary Education.* ASHE-ERIC Higher Education Report No. 3. Washington, D.C.: Association for the Study of Higher Education, 1987. (ED 286 437)

Naylor, M. *Articulation Between Secondary or Postsecondary Vocational Education Programs and Proprietary Schools.* ERIC Digest No. 64. Columbus, Ohio: ERIC Clearinghouse on Adult, Career, and Vocational Education, 1987. (ED 282 095)

New England Association of Schools and Colleges, Commission on Technical and Career Institutions. *Standards of Membership for Specialized Institutions of Higher Education Awarding an Associate Degree at the Technical and Career Level.* Winchester, Mass.: New England Association of Schools and Colleges, 1993.

Peterson, J. H. "Community College and Proprietary School Relationships Within the Educational Marketplace." In F. C. Kintzer (ed.), *Improving Articulation and Transfer Relationships.* New Directions for Community Colleges, no. 39. San Francisco: Jossey-Bass, 1982.

Prager, C. "Accreditation and Transfer: Mitigating Elitism." In B. W. Dziech and W. Vilter (eds.), *Prisoners of Elitism: The Community College's Struggle for Stature.* New Directions for Community Colleges, no. 78. San Francisco: Jossey-Bass, 1992.

Robertson-Smith, M. *Accreditation Models for Vocational Education.* Columbus, Ohio: ERIC Clearinghouse on Adult, Career, and Vocational Education, 1990. (ED 327 737)

Western Association of Schools and Colleges, Accrediting Commission for Community and Junior Colleges. *Handbook of Accreditation and Policy Manual: 1990 Edition.* Aptos, Calif.: Western Association of Schools and Colleges, 1990.

Young, K. E. "Accrediting Organizations: You Can't Tell the Players Without a Program." *Career Training,* 1987, 3 (3), 8–10.

CAROLYN PRAGER *is dean of the College of Arts and Sciences at Franklin University in Columbus, Ohio.*

The author identifies federal student aid policy as the primary driver of adaptive change in proprietary institutions and suggests that the essential differences between proprietary schools and community colleges remain.

The Illusion of Convergence: Federal Student Aid Policy in Community Colleges and Proprietary Schools

Richard W. Moore

In this chapter, I argue that the apparent convergence of community colleges and proprietary schools is in large part caused by changes in federal student aid policy. This apparent convergence masks real and profound differences between these institutions, which will persist and prevent any real convergence of the two sectors in the foreseeable future.

Illusion of Organic Convergence

From a distance, it is easy to make the case that community colleges and proprietaries are converging. Both sectors serve an increasing number of non-traditional students who are older and more likely to be minorities and economically disadvantaged. Both sectors are willing to enroll students who were not successful in high school (Apling, 1993). Many community colleges have joined proprietary schools in making vocational training the primary focus of their instructional program (Brint and Karabel, 1989). Community colleges are shortening their vocational programs and focusing on certificates rather than degrees, while proprietary school programs are getting longer and more schools are beginning to offer degrees. More proprietaries are seeking regional accreditation in order to offer transferable credit. These arguments for convergence have been made vigorously in other chapters.

A hidden assumption of those arguing that convergence is taking place is that the natural evolution of proprietary schools and community colleges moves them toward convergence. I call this the *organic convergence hypothesis*.

However, if we look at what is behind the changing behavior of these institutions, we see only marginal changes in community colleges. In proprietary schools, we see that federal student aid policy, which is aimed at reducing student loan defaults and eliminating fraud from student aid, is forcing proprietary schools into the mold of traditional institutions. I call this the *forced convergence hypothesis.*

Federal Student Aid Policy and Forced Convergence

Understanding the forced convergence hypothesis begins with an understanding of the powerful role federal student aid policy plays in shaping the behavior of proprietary schools. Virtually all proprietary schools enroll at least some students who receive federal student aid. Nationally, 79 percent of all proprietary students receive some federal aid, compared to 29 percent of all students (Fraas, 1990, p. 7). In some schools, up to 90 percent of the student tuition is paid by federal student aid. Changes in federal student aid eligibility policies were largely responsible for the proliferation of proprietary schools in low-income, inner-city areas in the 1970s and 1980s. The availability of federal student aid and the profits produced by enrolling aid-eligible students are primarily what fueled the rapid expansion of the proprietary sector in the 1980s and enticed many entrepreneurs into the sector.

On the other side of the equation, the fraud in student aid programs, combined with high default rates on guaranteed student loans and low completion and placement rates for low-income students receiving federal aid, triggered the continuing scandal within the sector. Recent changes in student aid policy, particularly in the area of guaranteed student loans, are largely responsible for the rapid contraction of the sector in the 1990s and the virtual disappearance of proprietary schools from inner-city areas in cities such as Los Angeles.

After a period of explosive growth in the 1980s, the proprietary sector is in a period of unprecedented turbulence. Schools are rapidly shifting their business strategies in response to the amendments to the Higher Education Act amendments of 1992 (P.L. 102–325) and the regulations that enforce it. Access to student loans has dried up for many schools with high default rates, and other schools have voluntarily left the program out of fear that a high default rate will eliminate them from other student aid programs, particularly Pell grants. The number of accredited schools that are eligible to participate in federal student loans is in sharp decline. For example, after years of growth, the number of schools accredited by the Accrediting Commission of Independent Colleges and Schools (ACICS) has declined from 1,022 in 1989 to 755 in 1992—a decline of 26 percent, according to ACICS. Most of these schools were so-called high-default schools located in urban areas that either lost their loan eligibility because of high default rates or were unable to find lenders willing to lend to their students because of high defaults. Some simply closed up before they lost eligibility or loan access. Several large chains of schools such as United Education and Software have gone into bankruptcy and closed a large number of campuses.

The amendments to the HEA of 1992 made a host of policy changes that are forcing proprietary schools to behave more like community colleges. For example, the number of clock hours is increased to 600—the minimum mandated program length to be eligible for student aid. Thus, proprietary schools are lengthening their programs and making them more like the traditionally longer community college programs. The regulations that support the Act prefer that programs be measured in credit hours rather than clock hours, causing many schools to shift to credit hours. The Act requires the proprietary schools to get at least 15 percent of their revenues from sources other than Title IV federal student aid. This provision discourages proprietaries from targeting low-income students exclusively and seeks to make them more like community colleges, which tend to have more diverse student populations and be less dependent on federal aid. The Act bars commission payments to admissions representatives, which changes a business practice within the sector that has persisted for over a century and again gives the appearance that proprietary admissions practices will now be more in the community college counseling mode than in the business-oriented sales mode. Regulations that inhibit branching and make it much more difficult to establish new campuses will limit the rapid expansion and contraction of proprietary school sites that have characterized the industry since 1972 and again give the schools more of the stability that is typical of the public sector.

While community colleges are subject to the same regulations as proprietary schools, these regulations have a much more limited impact on them. First, many fewer community college students receive federal student aid. For example, in 1986, 81 percent of proprietary school students received some federal aid, compared to only 34 percent of community college vocational students and 20 percent of community college students overall (Apling, 1993). Since tuition at community colleges is low, the bulk of the aid received goes to paying students' living expenses and thus is not really a source of revenue for colleges. Community colleges continue to get the bulk of their funding from government agencies. Most are part of a system in which they receive funding through statewide systems and local tax assessments, thus their focus is the state legislative and regulatory systems that determine the level of funding rather than some market mechanism.

The dramatically different role that federal student aid plays in the two sectors is best illustrated by what happens when a campus is declared ineligible for federal student aid because of high default rates on federal student loans. Many inner-city community colleges have lost aid eligibility, yet none of these schools have closed or moved. They remain in operation with the state and local funds they receive. Conversely, most proprietary schools that have lost their eligibility have closed, and some schools in danger of losing their eligibility have moved, seeking markets with students who are less likely to default on student loans.

Barriers to Organic Convergence

Regulators will never achieve the social goals they have for the schools by attempting to micromanage schools' behavior through student aid policy, because they fail to understand the profound differences that separate proprietary schools from community colleges. For several decades, organizational theorists have argued that the distinctions between public and private organizations have become blurred. Independent private organizations, such as housing nonprofits or community-based mental health facilities, often provide public goods, while some governmental agencies, such as the Post Office or the National Park Service, rely on private payment for services for most of their budget. Reviewing several decades of research on the distinctions between public and private organizations, Hal G. Rainey (1991) has this warning for researchers and managers:

> Theory, research, and the realities of the contemporary political economy show the inadequacy of simple notions about differences between public and private organizations. For management theory and research, this poses the challenge of determining what role a public-private distinction can play and how. For practical management and public policy, it means that we must avoid over simplifying the issue and jumping to conclusions about sharp distinctions between public and private (p. 14).

Rainey's analysis suggests that simple distinctions—assuming that community colleges are hierarchical, bureaucratic public agencies and that proprietary schools are purely autonomous market-driven enterprises—will not stand up to serious analysis. I believe he is correct. The clear distinctions that once separated proprietary schools from community colleges have become muddied over time but not to the degree that would warrant any reasonable expectation that the two sectors will converge in the foreseeable future.

Table 7.1 summarizes the key differences between community colleges and proprietary schools. A careful review of these differences shows that the appearance of convergence masks profound differences that will ensure that community colleges and proprietary schools remain distinct. The differences between these types of institutions begin with dramatically different missions. The community colleges have complex missions that at a minimum involve providing academic transfer programs, vocational education, remedial education, and community service. In addition, community colleges may offer contract training to local employers and distance learning to remote locations. Proprietary schools are driven by a single clear goal: to turn a profit for an owner, whether it is an individual, a partnership, or a group of corporate stockholders. While both types of institutions may seek growth, the reasons they wish to grow are different. Proprietaries will seek growth as long as the marginal cost of adding students is less than the marginal revenue additional students generate. Community colleges will seek growth to better serve their

Table 7.1. Differences Between Proprietary Schools and Community Colleges

Feature	Public Community Colleges	Proprietary Schools
Mission	Complex and ambiguous; includes: Academic transfer programs Vocational training Community service Remedial education Preserving the jobs and status of faculty and staff	Simple and focused aim: Profit for the owner, through offering short-term vocational training
Governance	Complex: Elected state and local boards State legislation Faculty governance State and federal regulation	Simple: Owners and professional managers State and federal legislation
Time horizon	Long term	Short term
Size	Large	Small
Links to the rest of higher education	Strong systematic ties through transferable credit and articulation with four-year institutions and other community colleges Usually part of a statewide system	Limited links to four-year institutions and other less-than-four-year institutions Transferability of credit is limited and ad hoc May be part of a local, regional, or national chain of schools with the same owner
Cost	Free or minimal tuition	Significant tuition of $4,000 or more for a vocational program
Market orientation	Has assigned territory in which it is the only community college Some funding usually driven by enrollment Some competition for enrollment with other public and private institutions	Has no assigned territory; moves to find markets Completely dependent on enrollments for revenue Competes with other proprietary and public institutions in market
	No need to differentiate itself from other institutions and establish a competitive advantage	Must differentiate itself from other public and private competitors to establish a competitive advantage that will warrant higher tuition charges

communities or to achieve status for the faculty and staff in the eyes of other institutions; thus, community colleges may seek growth, even when growth will generate more costs than revenue.

The behavior of both community colleges and proprietary schools is shaped by their governance structures, which are closely linked to their mission. The governance of community colleges is complex. The colleges themselves are often large, with thousands of students and dozens of departments, and they may be part of a statewide system with many campuses and tens of thousands of students. Community colleges are governed by one or more public boards that are elected or appointed at least in part to reflect the varied constituencies they must serve. The colleges are subject to state legislation, as well as regulation aimed specifically at them by the state legislatures that provide the bulk of the funding for most colleges (Cohen and Brawer, 1989). In addition, the colleges must comply with a host of state and federal regulations aimed at higher education in general. Finally, at the institutional level, faculty may play a significant role in the governance of the institution through faculty senates and various committees. In some states, powerful faculty unions shape policy at the board and legislative levels through political action. Thus, policy development in the community college sector is slow-moving, as complex negotiations take place at various levels among the many stakeholder groups. Once a college is established, it is likely to remain in place for decades. In fact, colleges seldom close or move. Thus, policy and planning goes forward with a long-term perspective.

Conversely, in proprietary schools governance is relatively simple. It primarily consists of the business decisions made by a school's owners and professional managers (Wilms, 1976). Faculty play a limited and informal role, if any, in policy decisions, and faculty unions are virtually unknown. Regulation of proprietary schools at the state level historically has been minimal, since few schools receive any state funding, and few states have devoted many resources to the regulation of proprietary schools, regardless of what rules are actually on the books (Chaloux, 1985).

The schools are subject to the same federal regulation as other institutions participating in federal student aid programs, and thus this regulation has become the primary policy intervention for controlling the behavior of proprietary schools. Because they are managed like businesses, proprietary schools operate within a much shorter time frame. Typically, business plans are developed and revised quarterly, while long-term planning seldom goes beyond a year or two. Short-term planning is practical in a business that must respond to shifting student preferences or go out of business. Proprietary schools open and close with such regularity that in a large state like California, it is even difficult to get an accurate count of schools.

Community colleges have strong systematic links to the rest of higher education. The community colleges serve as pipelines for local four-year institutions. Most community colleges are part of a statewide system of public two-year and four-year colleges and universities that has as a goal the easy movement of students between institutions. These arrangements are formalized through articulation agreements that ensure that work taken at the community college will meet requirements for four-year degrees at other institutions. Even without articulation agreements, credits from community colleges, almost all of which have regional accreditation, have a reasonable chance of transferring to other institutions that have accreditation from the same regional authority (Cohen and Brawer, 1987). On the other hand, most proprietary schools do not offer degrees and do not have regional accreditation. Thus, credits earned at proprietary schools are seldom transferable except when specific agreements are made with other, usually private, institutions (Lee and Merisotis, 1990, p. 14). If proprietary schools have close ties to other institutions, it is usually to other schools owned by the same owner to form a regional or national chain. Even in national chains, local schools often have a great deal of autonomy.

Perhaps the most important difference between proprietary schools and community colleges is their market orientation and cost. While recent hard economic times have caused many community colleges to raise tuition, community colleges remain higher education's open door and thus charge as little tuition as possible to keep their programs affordable. Historically, tuition generates a very small proportion of community colleges' revenues, and that proportion is usually stable. Cohen and Brawer (1989, p. 128) report that tuition made up 15 percent of community college revenue in 1975 and rose to only 16 percent in 1986.

Most colleges operate under some sort of financing system under which they are paid for student enrollments. More students mean more money, although in times of tight budgets, enrollments may be capped and funding reduced. Community colleges may also offer extension or community service programs for which the cost of instruction is paid by fees or tuition, while public funds cover the cost of overhead and administration. Thus, the colleges are responsive, to some degree, to the market and shifts in student preferences, but they remain principally driven by the notion of community service. To maintain enrollment, community colleges adopt behaviors formerly only found in the proprietary sector: they advertise aggressively; they develop course and program titles with a contemporary sound that will attract students; and recruiters visit local high schools and community-based organizations to recruit students.

However, other factors limit the ability of community colleges to be market-driven. Most colleges offer faculty tenure and thus make every effort to keep programs and faculty even when enrollment drops. In the vocational area, the colleges often make heavy investments in capital equipment that they have a hard time maintaining or disposing of if enrollments drop. Community colleges are usually assigned a territory, thus while they have a monopoly in their service area, they are unable to move geographically to seek new or better markets. Community colleges that have been successful in contract training, which is unsubsidized fee-for-service training with employers, have usually set up independent units that are free from the regulations that govern the regular program. They often do not use regular faculty, and often are located off campus. These programs also generate relatively small amounts of revenue. Cohen and Brawer (1989, p. 128) found that "auxiliary services" accounted for only 6 percent of community college income in 1986. This type of behavior could be considered evidence of convergence, but to me it shows how peripheral market-oriented programs are to the core activities of community colleges.

Proprietary schools are completely dependent on enrollments for revenue. Whether the money comes from federal student aid or from tuition the student pays out of his or her own pocket, without enrollments there is no revenue. Thus, proprietary schools devote a tremendous amount of time, energy, and money to recruiting and retaining students.

A study of Maryland proprietary schools found that advertising alone made up 11 percent of all school expenditures. A separate study of proprietary business schools reports that the total cost of student recruitment was 18 percent of all expenditures (Apling and Aleman, 1990). A proprietary school director usually has a weekly enrollment count, and an enrollment forecast that is adjusted weekly as well. To keep enrollments up, proprietary schools are quick to add, drop, and modify programs to respond to student preferences (Wilms, 1976). If markets decline, proprietary schools will close up and move on. If markets are growing, the schools will branch out and open new campuses rapidly.

Perhaps most importantly, proprietaries must charge a substantial tuition to pay for the cost of training and generate a profit. To warrant the additional amount they charge beyond the cost of a similar community college program, proprietaries must create some added value for the customer, in this case the student, which is worth the extra cost, or they will simply go out of business.

Proprietary schools employ several business strategies to add value and to differentiate themselves from and achieve a competitive advantage over community colleges. Proprietary schools usually offer shorter programs, lowering the cost of attending by reducing the income that is foregone while attending, and making the goal of a job seem more immediate. In proprietary schools, students may enter every month or six weeks rather than waiting for the start of a semester or quarter, thus making enrolling more convenient. The schools may offer programs that do not exist in community colleges, such as optical dispensing, truck driving, or cosmetology. Schools may add value by supplying smaller classes or more aggressive placement at graduation. Perhaps most important, proprietary schools lavish individual attention on students. Students who are absent for several days will be called at home by instructors. Admissions representatives help students overcome barriers that may keep them from attending, whether it is figuring out bus schedules or making daycare arrangements. Faculty are held accountable for retaining students in their classes and carefully monitoring their progress (Wilms, 1987). For students who have not been successful in traditional institutions, the very fact that the proprietary school environment and organizational culture is business-like and not school-like may provide a value for which they will pay. In short, proprietary schools cannot converge with community colleges, because to do so would be to lose their competitive advantage and hence their ability to charge enough tuition to survive.

Forecast

As Rainey suggests, the distinctions between proprietary schools and community colleges are not as clear-cut as theorists might once have believed. However, further analysis shows that real and profound differences between these institutions do persist despite federal policies that have created the illusion of convergence. The final regulations to implement the amendments to the HEA of 1992 are just being released as this chapter is written. Their long, controversial journey is due in part to the federal government's drive to force proprietary schools into the mold of traditional institutions, and in so doing, the federal government has put stricter limits on the behavior of other types of institutions as well (Leatherman, 1993).

It seems that the most immediate effect of the new law is not so much to force a convergence between proprietary schools and traditional institutions but simply to reduce the number of proprietary schools. At the same time, the federal government's new direct-lending program is likely to restore access to federal student loans for a large number of proprietary schools that have had trouble getting access to student loans through private banks. Another enrollment boom may be generated in the proprietary sector (Moore, 1994). What continues to be missing from federal student aid policy directed at proprietary schools is a clear understanding that they are driven by different incentives than traditional institutions. Rather than attempt to micromanage proprietary schools in what appears to be a futile effort to force them into the mold of traditional institutions, policy makers need to design policies that tap the incentives that drive the schools to achieve social goals. A student aid system that made payment of aid contingent upon desired outcomes—program completion and placement in a related job—would be a giant step forward.

The long-term consequences of the federal drive to shape proprietary schools in the image of traditional higher education remain uncertain, but the chances that proprietary schools and community colleges will converge into a single institutional type seem slim indeed.

References

Apling, R. N. "Proprietary Schools and Their Students." *Journal of Higher Education,* 1993, *64,* 379–416.

Apling, R. N., and Aleman, S. R. *Proprietary Schools: A Description of Institutions and Students.* Congressional Research Service Report for Congress 90–428 EPW. Washington, D.C.: Library of Congress, 1990.

Brint, S., and Karabel, J. *The Diverted Dream: Community Colleges and the Promise of Educational Opportunity in America 1890–1985.* New York: Oxford University Press, 1989.

Chaloux, B. "State Oversight of the Private and Proprietary Sector." Paper presented at a joint session of the National Association of Trade and Technical Schools and the Association of Independent Colleges and Schools, Miami, Fla., Apr. 19, 1985. (ED 270 060)

Cohen, A. M., and Brawer, F. B. *The Collegiate Function of Community Colleges: Fostering Higher Learning Through Curriculum and Student Transfer.* San Francisco: Jossey-Bass, 1987.

Cohen, A. M., and Brawer, F. B. *The American Community College.* (2nd ed.) San Francisco: Jossey-Bass, 1989.

Fraas, C. J. *Proprietary Schools and Student Financial Aid Programs: Background and Policy Issues.* Washington, D.C.: Congressional Research Service, Library of Congress, 1990.

Leatherman, C. "Proposed Regulations on Accrediting Groups Draw Angry Response." *Chronicle of Higher Education,* Aug. 4, 1993, p. 23.

Lee, J. B., and Merisotis, J. P. *Proprietary Schools: Programs, Policies, and Prospects.* ASHE-ERIC Higher Education Report No. 5. Washington, D.C.: School of Education and Human Development, George Washington University, 1990. (ED 331 337)

Moore, R. W. "Proprietary Schools and Direct Lending." In *Selected Issues in the Federal Direct Loan Program: A Collection of Commissioned Papers.* Washington, D.C.: U.S. Department of Education, Office of the Under Secretary and Office of Postsecondary Education, 1994.

Rainey, H. G. *Understanding and Managing Public Organizations.* San Francisco: Jossey-Bass, 1991.

Wilms, W. W. *Public and Proprietary Vocational Training: A Study of Effectiveness.* New York: Lexington Books, 1976.

Wilms, W. W. "Proprietary Schools: Strangers in Their Own Land?" *Change,* 1987, Jan–Feb, 10–21.

RICHARD W. MOORE *is professor in the School of Business Administration and Economics, California State University, Northridge.*

State oversight is a response to demands for accountability for student achievement and for the use of student financial aid; the overall effect may be a forced convergence.

State Oversight of the Proprietary Sector

Bruce N. Chaloux

The role of the states in the oversight of postsecondary education resembles, in many instances, a patchwork quilt. It is a quilt of fifty-one pieces (fifty states and the District of Columbia), each unique in structure and scope. Despite the lack of similarity among the states, and despite claims that the autonomy of the states is the stitching for this patchwork quilt of high-quality public and private postsecondary education, many argue that there does exist a national "system" of higher education.

While community colleges have a clearly defined place and status in the family of institutions of higher education, this is not the case with the majority of proprietary schools. Nowhere are these differences among states more prominent than in the oversight of the proprietary sector. The proprietary sector remains an enigma to many state higher education agencies and poses many problems for state planners. Although the educational objectives of the community colleges and institutions in the proprietary sector seem, in many instances, to be the same, the state's treatment of these institutions is markedly different. The reasons for this are varied.

A continuing and fundamental problem is the lack of a common definition for proprietary education. Wittstruck's (1985) study, "State Oversight of Degree Granting Authority in Proprietary Institutions," reveals a variety of definitions among states, ranging from "for profit" (the most common) to no specific definition. Often, the states refer to occupational or trade and technical schools as proprietary, whether or not the institutions are for-profit operations. The more popular current title, and most descriptive—career schools—has yet to be insinuated into most state's regulatory vocabulary.

The profit motive, or the notion of education being a business, remains a difficult concept for many in the traditional sectors of higher education to accept. Many consider this motive incongruous with the goals and objectives of education, suggesting that the profitability of an operation is often gained by sacrifices in the quality of the educational product. There is little doubt that state higher education agencies have historically been troubled by this financial objective, believing that sound academic principles and the historical nature and traditions of higher education can, and are, often compromised by owners of the for-profit institutions (Lee and Merisotis, 1990).

Other problems are tied directly to the perception that proprietary schools are more closely aligned with secondary education than with postsecondary education. This view is supported by state regulatory approaches to proprietary institutions, in which responsibility for oversight is often assigned to state departments of education and not to state higher education coordinating or governing bodies. Conversely, the proprietary sector views itself as an important player in postsecondary education, enrolling thousands of students annually and providing important and needed educational services. The proprietary sector argues that the profit motive is misunderstood and that the quality of the educational product, as measured by the successful placement and work results of its students, is not given full or appropriate recognition.

Somehow, the proprietary sector has failed to communicate the nature of its activities to the states, and states have generally excluded the proprietary sector from higher education planning processes. There is a general lack of understanding and a major communication problem for both. This is particularly perplexing, given that the students served by both community colleges and the career schools are often indistinguishable (Lee, 1990).

Although recent concerns about the proprietary sector and the role of the states has focused primarily on issues relating to student loan defaults, there are many issues and concerns about the proprietary sector that are longstanding and relate to the roles of the states, the federal government, and private accreditation. These roles have changed dramatically over the past thirty years. The players in this oversight triad are inexorably linked in a delicate balance. More recently, imbalance has set in and the evolving role of the states is both intriguing and disquieting to many in higher education.

Oversight Triad: Roles and Responsibilities

The traditional role of the states in postsecondary education is long-established. That role is to oversee the postsecondary educational activities within its boundaries and to coordinate, plan, approve, and authorize such activities as the state's legislative body may direct by statute. This role is undertaken by either governing or coordinating boards, the former having more direct authority and control over all curricular and fiscal matters (for example, New York's State Board of Regents), the latter having more planning and coordinating functions (for example, Virginia's State Council of Higher Education). Although there are variations of these two forms of statewide structures, all states have some body or bodies charged with such planning and policy development efforts.

The federal role in postsecondary education has traditionally been limited but has increased dramatically during the period following the Second World War, first with the G.I. Bill, which provided support for and access to higher education for hundreds of thousands of soldiers returning from conflict, and then by providing federal support for facilities expansion, financial aid, and other initiatives to deal with the so-called baby boom generation from this same group of veterans. Following this massive growth period in the 1960s and early 1970s, the federal role began to change, most specifically with the passage of the amendments to the Higher Education Act of 1972, which, among a variety of new initiatives, mandated a broader role for states in postsecondary planning. Many in the proprietary sector believed at the time that this federal action had given them a seat at higher education's table. Little did the proprietary sector realize how costly and uncomfortable this seat would be.

The third partner in the triad, the voluntary private accrediting community, has been a somewhat unwilling partner in this oversight effort. The federal government chose to rely on private accreditation rather than governmental accreditation as a means of determining eligibility for federal student aid and assuring the quality and integrity of higher education. Whether desired or not—and many groups and reports have called for the separation of federal student aid eligibility from the accreditation process—it has remained in effect and, for the most part, unchanged, until very recently.

State Oversight: Historical Context

Until the 1960s and early 1970s, statewide governing or coordinating boards had little or no involvement with the proprietary sector. This changed dramatically in the 1960s, as postsecondary education entered the "golden age" of higher education. Changes included massive increases in the number of students attending college, hundreds of new institutions, major facilities expansion on existing campuses, and significant curricular changes and program growth. For the most part, state higher education agencies played a direct role in nurturing growth while maintaining concern for quality education during this period.

The growth in the public sector forced many proprietary institutions to seek alternative means for maintaining enrollments. During this period, many for-profit institutions sought to add degree programs to properly validate student learning experiences and to provide credential-conscious students with an accepted academic diploma. The proprietary sector also sought access to the huge federal support that students in more traditional institutions were receiving. Indeed, proprietary institutions were successful in their efforts on both counts, but in reaching these goals new and difficult problems arose with both state agencies and the accrediting community.

Another effort by the proprietary sector and, in fact, many private institutions, was to bring educational services to the student in the home, workplace, or other non-campus-based location. The period witnessed explosive growth in outreach activities, including many off-campus, out-of-state, and out-of-region instructional programs. In contrast, most state-supported institutions, faced with tremendous growth and development of their campuses, did little to move programs off campus. Instead, they moved toward the development of entire systems of community colleges that would provide access for everyone.

These changes altered the traditional approaches to access and availability of higher education programs and services. Not surprisingly, a number of marginal-quality, and even unacceptable-quality operations were developed during this period. A good number of these were proprietary in nature but were not institutions designed specifically to provide programming and to profit from the effort. Rather, they were shoddy diploma mills that sold academic credentials to a credential-conscious and demanding public. Whether fair or not, the proprietary sector bore the brunt of criticism and became a target for many in the higher education establishment.

Many have blamed the lack of adequate state oversight for the growth of diploma mills, correctly citing that the states traditionally have been legally responsible for authorizing educational activity within state boundaries (Bender and Davis, 1972). But prior to the 1970s, most states were not faced with the problem of institutional oversight in their own state. Not surprisingly, the states' reaction was to develop new laws, regulations, and standards to review private degree-granting institutions. This was accomplished with the help of the federal government, which, in the amendments to the HEA of 1972, extended eligibility for federal assistance to many post-high school programs, institutions, and other educational operations. Section 1202 of the amendments states that "any State which desires to receive assistance under section 1203 or Title X shall establish a State Commission or designate an existing State agency or State Commission which is broadly and equitably representative of the general public and private nonprofit and proprietary institutions of postsecondary education in the State" (U.S. Committee on Education and Labor, 1979).

By the mid 1970s, most states had established "1202 Commissions" for carrying out the planning mandate of the amendments to the HEA of 1972. These commissions were created to ensure comprehensive statewide planning. However, with the extended eligibility for student financial aid came the problem of ferreting out the viable, ethical educational endeavors from those with a dubious orientation. This task fell in part to state licensing agencies, which, as noted earlier, were only beginning to develop strategies for dealing with this set of problems.

During the 1970s and early 1980s, a number of initiatives and efforts were undertaken to assist states in dealing with the new roles and responsibilities and specifically with the proprietary sector. The following are worthy of note:

Education Commission of the States (ECS) "model legislation." Responding to state needs for help in creating and enacting statutes or amendments to deal with the escalating problem of inferior institutional quality, the model legislation offered a broad set of provisions for use by states in the oversight of post-secondary institutions and was very much consumer-oriented. This report may be the single most influential document on the licensing process for state agencies. To this day, it is a basic resource for states developing or revising their laws and regulations (Education Commission of the States, 1973).

Airlie House Conference (1975). This conference was the first national effort to review various problems and approaches to the state licensing of private degree-granting institutions. It became a springboard for a broader national discussion. Even so, many of the issues discussed at this conference are still unresolved, including the problem of states having no licensing laws or having inadequate regulations, the lack of a national clearinghouse for information about institutions operating in more than one state, and the general absence of definition regarding the roles of states and the accrediting community in ensuring institutional integrity and quality (Postsecondary Education Convening Authority, 1975).

Keystone Conference (1976). This conference was an effort of the now-defunct Postsecondary Education Convening Authority to bring together representatives from the states, accrediting agencies, and the federal government to rekindle the triad concept of partnership and cooperation concerning institutional approval, accreditation, and eligibility. Although a number of tangible, significant outcomes from that conference remain, including formal networks such as Persons Responsible for Oversight Activities of Non-Public Degree-Granting Institutions (PROANDI) and less formal communication linkages, no formal policies for cooperative arrangements were developed (Marchese, 1976). Many have called for a second Keystone conference, believing that changes in the roles of the triad partners since 1976 would foster new and beneficial progress. Lack of funding, coordination, and interest have precluded a sequel.

Project ALLTEL (1982–1984). This project was a joint effort of the then-Council on Postsecondary Accreditation and the State Higher Education Executive Officers (SHEEO), that focused on the assessment of distance learning via telecommunications. The issue of a state's authority to license or approve activities that were interstate in nature and that used some form of technological delivery mechanism was of particular interest. Interestingly, the legal debate continues about the states' right to review and approve, even as new technologies provide increasing opportunities for reaching students (Chaloux, 1985a). Despite this effort, the relationships between state higher education agencies and accrediting bodies remains uneven.

Approaches to State Oversight

Many in higher education believe that the states' "desire" is to police education within their boundaries. Many also view this behavior as the "intrusion of state governments into what has historically been the province of collegial accrediting bodies" (Clohan, 1985). Many state officials would argue that their role increased only after the failure of the accrediting process to provide adequate protection for the educational consumer. These arguments do not alter the fact that since the 1980s, most states are, in fact, in the business of proprietary oversight.

States use a variety of approaches in licensing and authorizing institutions to operate and grant degrees in their jurisdictions. The three primary approaches are minimum standards, honest practice, and realization of objectives, although some states use a combination of these approaches (Chaloux, 1985b). With the minimum standards approach, a state agency evaluates whether an institution meets specified criteria at prescribed levels—for example, a certain number of library materials, full-time faculty, laboratory facilities, and classroom space. It is not unlike the approach used by accrediting agencies. The honest practice methodology is used to determine whether an institution fulfills claims made to the public. It is most concerned with such issues as reliability and accuracy of published materials and the adequacy of refund policies and other consumer protection measures. The realization of objectives methodology asks the questions: Has the institution set reasonable objectives? Does it have the potential for achieving those objectives?

By far the most popular approach is the minimum standards approach, which requires an institution to meet a prescribed set of standards and criteria that are not unlike those employed by accrediting agencies. In fact, the state's use of minimum standards fostered in the late 1960s and early 1970s by the off-campus activities noted earlier and the ECS model legislation is at the heart of many of the concerns about state oversight activities of the accrediting community.

The number of agencies in a single state that are charged with some aspect of regulating postsecondary education in their state only adds further confusion about state practices and interferes with comprehensive statewide planning (Wallhaus, 1985). This is particularly true for the proprietary sector, whose institutions are faced with satisfying the requirements of agencies ranging from the SHEEO office to the Department of Motor Vehicles (Chaloux, 1985b).

For traditional degree-granting institutions of higher education, states have either governing or coordinating agencies often referred to as the "SHEEO agency," which is typically responsible for statewide planning and coordination of higher education and, in many instances, has some regulatory responsibilities, either for authorizing the granting of degrees or regulating who can award degrees. The SHEEO agency is usually not responsible for non–degree-granting institutions, the category that most proprietary schools have traditionally occupied. This moves oversight of the for-profit, career-oriented schools into a hodge-podge of different state entities, usually linked to the kind of educational program the training focuses on. Thus, the range of state agency involvement encompasses the State Department of Education or an equivalent body and any number of specialized state agencies including health, transportation, and labor (Lee and Merisotis, 1990).

While all fifty states and the District of Columbia have some form of licensure or authorization procedures for proprietary schools, there is great divergence among the states as to how they act or treat various kinds of institutions (Lee and Merisotis, 1990). For example, some allow exemptions on the basis of regional or national accreditation or exclude those institutions operating on military establishments and religious institutions. Arguably, only forty states may be considered to have effective oversight procedures in place today—a continuing problem and concern for all states.

Evaluative Criteria in State Oversight

The nature of state oversight for degree-granting institutions is quite different from that for non–degree-granting institutions. Nowhere is this more evident than in the evaluative criteria used by states in assessing proprietary institutions. Generally, evaluation of degree-granting institutions focuses mainly on qualitative concerns and the educational validity of the activity. Although this is present to some extent in the non–degree-granting sector, the concern for consumer protection is far more prevalent.

While specific criteria that states use to evaluate an institution vary significantly, a general framework emerges from an analysis of state regulation. The categories most often found in state regulations are purposes and objectives, administration and governance, finance, curriculum, faculty, physical plant, library, student services, admissions and refund policy, publications, and college records (Chaloux, 1985a).

Most states have developed criteria that reflect the occupational specialties of programs and instruction for different types of institutions. These criteria emphasize the employability of the student upon completion of training, up-to-date training methods and instructional equipment, and vocational competencies for entry into the job market. Many states address the proprietary nature of the institutions by placing a special emphasis on disclosure of information. Advertising, promotional literature, catalogs, and other institutional information are all scrutinized for false or misleading statements. This emphasis on truth in advertising often follows Federal Trade Commission standards (Jung, Hamilton, Helliwell, and Wheeler, 1976).

Requirements for non–degree-granting and degree-granting institutions differ significantly in the financial area, in particular the bonding requirements to protect the rights of students. Tuition refund policies are closely monitored, and many states require institutions to post large bonds to protect students if programs are discontinued or institutions close. Many states also require agents of institutions to be bonded and licensed.

Clearly, the evaluative criteria for non–degree-granting institutions reflects the consumer movement of the 1970s, when a few proprietary schools were cited for abuses. The attendant publicity called attention to fraudulent practices and abuses in this sector of postsecondary education. Despite the efforts of federal, state, nongovernmental accrediting bodies and various associations, concerns about quality in the proprietary sector remain. Further evidence of this concern can be found in the 1991 study and report by the State Higher Education Executive Officers (1991) on proprietary institutions, undertaken to find ways to sharpen the states' response to the proprietary sector. The study points to the renewed interest in proprietary institutions and challenges posed by them for state agencies. The report suggested a significant turn away from a single "model" approach to a "models of good state practice," which recognizes the many differences in state approaches to licensing. The study's fundamental conclusion was that whatever governance model a state might choose to employ, "state licensing practices and procedures [must] be significantly reformed . . . [and] this reform must come in many forms, including staffing, the methods of paying for oversight, the inclusion of proprietary schools in the oversight process, and the many broad provisions concerned with consumer protections and education standards, such as advertising, institutional finances, and admissions standards" (State Higher Education Executive Officers, 1991, p. 76).

As more proprietary schools move to degree-granting status, new challenges are emerging for the states. The degree/non-degree classification system allowed many states to move oversight to nonacademic agencies that are often tied to the nature of the program to be reviewed. The awarding of traditional academic degrees by proprietary schools alters this arrangement and requires that the higher education oversight agency take responsibility for quality assurance. This may be, for many in the proprietary sector, a double-edged sword. On the one hand, recognition as a higher education institution is both positive and fulfilling. On the other hand, the longstanding and deeply held views of the proprietary sector and the traditional and inflexible standards that will be applied to these new degree-granting operations will create many problems. The recent SHEEO study suggests, at the very least, a need to broaden the understanding of proprietary institutions. This effort is commendable, but other efforts in the past have failed to produce the desired results, and it is still too early to assess the impact of the 1991 study.

Interestingly, and somewhat ironically, there is a shift underway in most states toward assessment strategies and measures for the accountability and efficacy of traditional higher education programming. As higher education continues to struggle with working in an environment of diminishing resources, more states are seeking data from traditional institutions on job placement, student performance on national exams, and assessments of the need for various programs. The irony is that the proprietary sector has historically collected and made available this information to its customers, believing that the single best measure of quality is whether students, after completing a program of some kind, can get employment in that field and can successfully perform their duties. The move from traditional input measures to more output measures by states can only be effective, however, if the traditional measures are altered significantly. Collecting data on retention and completion rates, job placement rates, skill assessment, and other output measures can only be effective if all institutions—public, private, and proprietary—are held to acceptable standards and that these standards are applied equitably to all educational institutions. The former can be achieved; the latter will require significant changes in the understanding of and perceptions (and biases) about proprietary schools by state higher education leaders.

A New Era: State Postsecondary Review Entities

The amendments to the HEA of 1992 contained provisions to create State Postsecondary Review Entities, or SPREs, as they have become commonly known. The impetus for this legislation was the increasing misuse of federal aid, particularly by the proprietary sector, where loan default rates have soared during the 1980s. Many have pointed a finger at Congress for this mess, noting that it was their decision to extend eligibility to the proprietary sector in the 1970s without proper safeguards to ensure repayment. Whoever was responsible, the media have provided story after story of misuse, abuse, and fraud within the system ranging from the enrollment of prisoners to the falsification of records and signing up nonexistent students to pad enrollments. After bilking the federal government, these educational entrepreneurs would close up shop, move their operations, change institutional names, or take other evasive measures to stay ahead of federal regulators. Defaults of $2.5 billion annually finally caused a rethinking of the problem and a call for new solutions. Part of the solution was the establishment of the SPREs as a "weapon to attack fraud and abuse," according to David Longenacker, Assistant Secretary for Postsecondary Education (Longenacker, 1994).

The establishment of the SPREs vests a new degree of power in the states and consequently may limit institutional autonomy (National Association of State Universities and Land Grant Colleges, 1994). Aided by federal support, the SPREs would develop standards, or use existing minimum standards or baselines for academic and financial data (for example, graduation rates, withdrawal rates, placement information, licensure pass rates). The new law will set "triggers" to identify institutions that have serious academic or fiscal issues that the Department of Education would ask the SPRE to review. The triggers range from providing detailed information about programs, to presenting job placement prospects, to showing the relationship of tuition charges to salary expectations.

The SPRE review could result in the termination of an institution's eligibility to participate in federal aid programs. The Department of Education has indicated that it anticipates some 1,600 "problem schools" being reviewed in 1994 and another 2,800 in 1995. This dragnet approach, as some have labeled the effort, is viewed by many as intrusive and by most as an altering of the traditional role of the states and the voluntary accrediting community by making the latter part of a governmental regulatory activity (Davies, 1994).

It is unclear at this time how states will react, how effective the triggers will be, or even if this effort by the federal government to divert responsibilities to the states will meet the broader objectives set out in the law. What is known is that the states' responses have been varied, ranging from enthusiasm for the new regulatory role to disdain and a desire not to become the federal government's enforcement arm for programs it neither sought nor necessarily desired. Others in the academic community fear onerous data collection and oversight intrusion by the states, including the private sector that has traditionally had only minimal involvement and little direct responsibility to the states, with some exceptions (for example, New York). For the proprietary sector, the new state responsibilities will undoubtedly alter how they conduct their business and, in the worst case scenario, whom they serve (Davies, 1994). Any termination of eligibility for federal aid will have a dramatic negative impact on institutions, whether large or small. Such an action would, in all likelihood, force many to cease operations. Further, proprietary institutions that operate in more than one state will be facing different policies, procedures, and relationships with different state agencies, causing further difficulty for these institutions.

Clearly, the proprietary institutions have made it to the table. Many may soon question whether the meal is worth the trouble or even if the cost of dining with the traditional institutions can be justified.

The Technology Revolution

The newest challenge to state higher education agencies is the rapidly increasing use of technology to deliver educational services. Telecommunications technology may well have an impact similar to that of the off-campus explosion of the late 1960s and early 1970s. Many proprietary institutions—those that grant degrees and those that do not—have turned or may soon turn to technology to provide greater educational services to a wider range of students. Again, the states and the accrediting bodies will be challenged to ensure the quality and integrity of these educational activities and will face a new set of programming dynamics for which contemporary standards and criteria may not be appropriate.

Technology delivery systems pose unique challenges that may force significant changes in the relationship between state oversight agencies and accrediting bodies. The most significant challenge is the problem of "physical presence," defined as the degree of activity taking place in the state. As this term becomes more precisely defined by the courts, it will become the central issue upon which state regulation of telecommunications will be shaped. Traditionally, physical presence has been measured by the number of facilities, the presence of faculty, and the degree of classroom instruction (Chaloux, 1985a). But technologies such as the "information super highway," satellite-based programs such as those offered by the National Technological University, and cable's Mind Extension University, a proprietary academic endeavor of Jones InterCable, will alter traditional views and render current practices obsolete, ineffective, and quite possibly, illegal. Such changes may require new reciprocal agreements among the states, more formal procedures for sharing of information, and a stronger working relationship with the accrediting community.

The technology revolution will also test SPRE activities, by challenging traditional means for counting students, how services are provided (and where), and financial aid programs. Given the interest and experience of the proprietary sector in the use of technology to deliver instruction, it can be expected that institutions, state agencies, and the accrediting community will be pressed to develop new strategies for assessing quality and to adjust long-standing standards and approaches to determining quality.

Conclusion

Despite a long history of providing postsecondary educational services to millions of people, the proprietary sector remains a mystery to many state higher education agencies and generally falls outside of statewide higher education planning efforts. This is likely to change with the advent of SPREs and the new roles of the federal government, the accrediting community, and the states. Although it is impossible to define what the changes might be, it is clear that proprietary institutions will be faced with new and greater demands to demonstrate the value and quality of their educational programming. Still, the philosophical issue of education being a for-profit activity remains outside the mainstream. Whatever quality proprietary institutions might achieve, even if such quality is measured against traditional standards, it will be difficult to overcome this bias on the part of many in the higher education establishment.

In his opening chapter, Darrel Clowes spoke metaphorically of the medieval castle and characterized the proprietary institutions as "trappers in the hills . . . hunting and gathering, trying to stay alive." It is an intriguing metaphor, particularly with respect to the states' role and what is clearly emerging in higher education. To carry the metaphor further, the states have only been concerned about the activities in and around the castle, sought only to protect those at those strategic places, and cared little for those in the hills and distant parts. Today, however, those near the fortified city are looking outward to the trappers who bring new and exciting nourishment. As these changes take place, the states must move forward to ensure that their roles are balanced and fair and that these new ways of providing education, by whomever provides it and for whatever their motives, focuses on quality. Absent such changes, many from the fortified city may move toward the hills, where the trappers have devised innovative and creative means for satisfying the new demands of the citizens.

References

Bender, L. W., and Davis, J. A. *Danger: Will External Degrees Reincarnate Bogus Degree Mills? A Challenge to State and National Agencies.* Tallahassee, Fla.: Center for State and Regional Leadership, 1972.

Chaloux, B. N. *Project ALLTEL: A Summary Report*. Washington, D.C.: Council on Postsecondary Accreditation, State Higher Education Executive Officers Association, 1985a.

Chaloux, B. N. *State Oversight of the Private and Proprietary Sector*. Denver: State Higher Education Executive Officers Association, 1985b.

Clohan, W. Remarks in *Compass*, the newsletter of the Association of Independent Colleges and Schools, March 1985.

Davies, G. K. "Muddled Priorities on Loan Defaults." *Chronicle of Higher Education*, May 11, 1994, p. 52.

Education Commission of the States. *Model State Legislation: A Report of the Task Force*. Denver: Amendments to the Higher Education Act of 1965 (1972) P.L. 92–318, 1973.

Jung, S., Hamilton, J., Helliwell, C., and Wheeler, J. *Improving the Consumer Protection Function in Postsecondary Education. Final Technical Report*. Washington, D.C.: U.S. Department of Health, Education, and Welfare, Office of Education, 1976.

Lee, J. B. *Enrollment Sequences of Private Career School Students*. Washington, D.C.: Career Training Foundation, 1990.

Lee, J. B., and Merisotis, J. P. *Proprietary Schools: Programs, Policies, and Prospects*. ASHE-ERIC Higher Education Report No. 5. Washington, D.C.: School of Education and Human Development, George Washington University, 1990. (ED 331 337)

Longenacker, D. Remarks at the Association for Counselor Education and Supervision/National Center for Education Statistics Panel on Postsecondary Education, Washington, D.C., May 1994.

Marchese, T. *Synthesis of the Keystone Workshop for State Licensing and Approving Officials*. Washington, D.C.: Institute for Educational Leadership, George Washington University, 1976.

National Association of State Universities and Land Grant Colleges. "Universities Fear Threat to Autonomy." *Newsline*, Jan. 1994, pp. 4–5.

Postsecondary Education Convening Authority. *Approaches to State Licensing of Private Degree-Granting Institutions: The Airlie Conference Report*. Washington, D.C.: Institute for Educational Leadership, George Washington University, 1975.

State Higher Education Executive Officers. *The Methods and Effectiveness of State Licensing of Proprietary Institutions*. Denver: State Higher Education Executive Officers Association, 1991.

U.S. Committee on Education and Labor. *Higher Education Act of 1965 and Related Statutes*. Washington, D.C.: U.S. Government Printing Office, 1979.

Wallhaus, R. A. *Statewide Planning and Policy Development in Relation to Proprietary Schools*. Denver: State Higher Education Executive Officers Association, 1985.

Wittstruck, J. R. *State Oversight of Degree-Granting Authority in Proprietary Institutions: Report of a SHEEO Survey*. Denver: State Higher Education Executive Officers Association, 1985.

BRUCE N. CHALOUX *is associate dean of the graduate school at Virginia Polytechnic Institute and State University in Blacksburg, Virginia.*

*The author reviews the arguments presented and tentatively concludes
that convergence is more apparent than real, but that if external
pressures continue or increase, it may become reality.*

Proprietary Schools and Community Colleges: The Next Chapter

Elizabeth M. Hawthorne

Darrel Clowes shared a feudal-age metaphor depicting higher education in
which the proprietary schools as the hunters and gatherers were far outside
the castle keep, and the community colleges were outside the castle walls in
the villages around the castle. He artfully put forth the hypothesis that community colleges and career colleges are becoming more and more alike as the
hunters and gatherers make incursions into the villages and adopt many of
their customs, while the villagers ape some of the practices of the hunters and
gatherers.

Each author has addressed a different aspect of community colleges and
proprietary schools. Some have supported Clowes's thesis, and others have not.
With the exception of faculty (about which data on the proprietary sector are
sadly wanting), the authors outlined points of intersection and deviation that
give us all pause to consider what the next chapter may be for the connections
between the two sectors of postsecondary education.

Ever the Twain Shall Meet?

While these two sectors of postsecondary education may look more and more
alike, they are inherently different to the core. While evidence offered by the
authors does build a picture of proprietary schools that have increasingly begun
to look and behave like community colleges, these changes have been wrought
by external forces. External forces include federal requirements for eligibility
for student financial aid and thus accreditation, and states that treat the proprietary schools more like educational endeavors than businesses. Indeed, some

NEW DIRECTIONS FOR COMMUNITY COLLEGES, no. 91, Fall 1995   © Jossey-Bass Publishers of the changes have transformed for-profit trade schools into not-for-profit colleges. Still, those career colleges that remain for-profit, non–degree-granting organizations remain inherently different in purpose, curriculum, students, and often size from community colleges.

Neither for the community college nor for the career college are these changes evolutionary and natural outcomes of their missions. Thus, while they may look more and more alike, the two kinds of institutions are not more and more alike. If external forces cause them to become more alike than different, what are we losing of the distinctiveness of the proprietary sector and its contribution to American society? And of what choices may we be depriving students?

The fact is that traditional educators will always question the motives of career colleges whose purpose is to make money. As has become evident in the chapters in this volume, these two sectors clearly exhibit some related features; however, there is one fundamental difference between career colleges and community colleges: the former are in education to make money, and the latter accept money to provide education. This is a matter of values that drive decisions concerning admissions, curriculum, and selection of faculty; the overlap that may occur is more by chance than by design. These institutions are so alien to one another in their basic values and assumptions that they could never become alike and only appear to behave alike to ensure survival.

When career colleges dip into the pot of federal financial aid money, it is an irritant to the traditional sector with a service focus. If we believe that the schools provide a service to society, then we do not want to wipe them out. If we believe that the schools are ripping off students and taxpayers through illegal and unethical practices, then the question is how do we approach that without forcing the schools to be something they are not? Furthermore, if we set the same expectations and regulations for such inherently different kinds of organizations, we may undermine both the quality of work and the institutional missions.

Outcome measures have been used for a long time by career colleges to sell their educational products. Community colleges only recently have been asked to provide these data. But a single-purpose vocational trade school is not like a comprehensive community or technical college to which students enter with many different purposes—and find many different alternatives. The majority of traditional career colleges provide job training, not education for life, for citizenship, or for culture. Painting traditional trade schools and community colleges with the same brush not only unnaturally forces community colleges to be something they are not and should not be, that is, job training agencies, it also forces the trade schools to alter the way they work, which may increase their costs without improving their quality.

One might argue that the increasing focus on certificates in community colleges undermines the educational (versus training) mission of community colleges and increases the gap between community colleges and the universities, and therefore binds the community colleges closer to the trade schools. That is not sufficient justification for treating community colleges like trade schools, nor should trade schools be treated as though they shared the same mission as community colleges. The slight overlap offers many opportunities for collaboration, but that does not support the notion that the institutions are more and more alike—that they are converging.

The career colleges can and should be encouraged to remain in the hinterlands hunting and gathering, building temporary shelters, and moving when necessary. The characteristics of proprietary schools allow them to provide services not likely to be provided by other educational institutions. That some career colleges have chosen to build in the village near the castle and settle down with other villages indicates that in some instances they have been co-opted by the simply traditional postsecondary education system through regulation and accreditation. Or they have found the new way of life to be attractive. Thus, the sectors may not be converging so much as individual career colleges have adopted new missions and ways of conducting themselves.

As noted above, the proprietary sector has fought for inclusion in the higher education community in order for its students to avail themselves of federal financial aid. They have become significant actors in the federal education lobby scene. Their position is inherently self-seeking to remain in the business of education and wanting the benefits of those whose mission is education. The proprietary schools' entrance into the education community has put traditional postsecondary education institutions in some jeopardy. The high default rate and the narrow educational focus of the proprietary schools makes them targets for cuts when cuts in federal aid to education are being made or when regulations are being imposed on postsecondary education. For example, the high default rates incurred by students in the career colleges has led to substantive regulation by the federal government that has profoundly affected community colleges (not to mention accreditation), often unfairly. And the active presence of the proprietaries in the higher education scene has raised serious questions about the suitability of essentially vocational (versus general) education. Although vocational education has become a significant aspect of community colleges and part of their menu of programs developed to meet community needs, it hardly makes community colleges resemble career colleges.

When all are treated alike, the failure of many proprietary schools to meet the standards of community colleges inappropriately puts the support for all such education at risk. If the proprietary schools wish to be part of the federal education scene, they need to share a common purpose with educational institutions. Given that they do not have this common mission, they should not be treated the same way educational institutions are treated and should be regulated for the protection of the consumers, as other businesses are subjected to government oversight. It is clear from this volume that there is only one reason why proprietary schools have begun to look like traditional postsecondary education institutions—federal regulation of student financial aid. It appears that policy makers at the federal and state levels have two basic choices with respect to proprietary schools: to treat them as educational organizations or as businesses. In every way, proprietary schools, whether called career colleges or otherwise, are still proprietary. They are private property and run for private gain, whether or not they are providing a public good. On that basis, governmental oversight should focus on the dominant features of these organizations and provide adequate information for the consumer to make informed choices and to prevent consumer abuse, much as it does in the production of food, medicine, and toys.

Ah, the Rub

Community colleges, by the sheer numbers of students enrolled, can be credited with increasing access to higher education for segments of society that heretofore had limited opportunities. Similarly, career colleges have increased access for segments of our population that have been severely underserved by higher education. Certainly, the demands of a highly technological and sophisticated economy require expanded access. The flexibility and adaptability of trade schools, as they link the curriculum with workplace needs, suggests the importance of such schools for social and economic equity in a democratic society, whatever the tradeoffs may be.

Another point of linkage but one far less-developed is that of transfer. The transfer issue becomes murky because the traditional sector has deemed that all accreditation is not equal and, for the most part, only regional accreditation earns transferability of credits from one institution to another. So in that sense, even accreditation—the potential integrator of postsecondary education—has not taken advantage of this opportunity, suggesting that accreditation is a gatekeeper.

We might inquire, why should all entry-level postsecondary education or training have to be transferable? If students are advised correctly and not misled, why should a training course at a proprietary school be credit-worthy at a college or university whose mission and purpose is substantively different from that of the trade school? Universities and colleges are not vocational education centers, despite the rhetoric. They are designed to educate students more broadly, and to dilute that mission would have serious consequences for society.

Views of cooperation between disparate organizations are presented in this volume for schools and colleges wishing to use limited resources more efficiently. Still, the differences between the kinds of organizations continue to steer the joint-driven vehicle, and the route is more like a winding country road than a superhighway. Even with the differences between sectors of postsecondary education, however, there are opportunities for working together, and there are conditions under which it is not even desirable for them to do so; maintaining distinctiveness may be a greater contribution than seeking similarities.

The demands made on career colleges by their accrediting associations are not the same as those made on community colleges—for example, records of satisfactory employment levels of graduates and demonstration of appropriate interventions for ability-to-benefit students. The Accrediting Commission of Independent Colleges and Schools and the Accrediting Commission of Career

Schools and Colleges of Technology are very concerned about these issues. A careful review of marketing is conducted during accreditation visits. There is still a lack of even-handed treatment of the for-profit schools and colleges that may be a legacy of the Colonial Era, when unscrupulous operators recruited unqualified students, provided inadequate training, and misled the public.

Raising questions about proprietary schools regarding community colleges, and vice versa, can prompt healthy discourse that could improve both types of institutions. For example, the drive toward accountability by the career college accreditors and the outcomes assessment orientation demanded by many state legislatures for higher education have raised similar questions across the spectrum of higher education within the moat. One might wish for more healthy discourse and less rapid response than is usually the case, however. This moves us onto another track from the one where institutional purpose and mission largely drove accreditation and public expectation. By including profit-driven schools with clear and specific missions—job training for employment—into the fold of higher education, accreditors and lawmakers alike have affected traditional higher education in negative ways by making them accountable for the employability of their graduates. This is simply not the purpose of higher education, although it is a highly beneficial and desirable—and unintended—outcome. The mission of traditional higher education is to educate the intellect and interests of its students and to treasure and mine ideas and knowledge for society. The accreditation process has not yet settled how to deal with the substantive difference between institutions with distinctly different missions. Further, the shifting sands of accreditation leave us wondering what tomorrow may bring.

Tomorrow and Tomorrow

Throughout this volume, we have looked at how both sectors operate, what each is like, and what public policy stances are possible regarding the career colleges and the community colleges. The observations in this chapter argue against the convergence theory and are couched in the context that higher education public policy should result in the protection of the public, stewardship of public funds, and the promotion of service to society.

Good public policy will foster differences among postsecondary education services to allow for greater access to education by more segments of society through the provision of diverse services for multiple purposes. Fostering differences allows institutions to focus their missions and thus be more efficient and effective in seeking to be what they say they wish to be.

Some of the discussions about convergence focused on specific courses of study, for example, baccalaureate degree-granting programs and partnerships among for-profit and not-for-profit trade schools. The unitary treatment of the two sectors is fascinating. We discuss community colleges as if community colleges across the country were all alike or at least similar; we treat career colleges in the same way. However, the variety within each sector is astonishing with respect to size, students served, curriculum, student services, even use of federal student financial aid funds. Even with the array of data we have on community colleges, we are at a loss for data that reflect the variations within community colleges; we know even less about career colleges. This void severely limits our understanding of either sector, much less our ability to analyze the relationships between them effectively. Additional scholarly inquiry should seek to fill the gap in our knowledge.

We set out to examine the ways in which those farthest from the castle keep have mimicked one another or sought to share in the leftovers from the castle. We have found some evidence for the argument that the proprietary sector has aped the community college. Also, the community college has adopted some of the practices of the proprietary sector. What is most interesting from the research presented in this volume is that the two sectors about which we write are not monolithic and that we know far too little to make wise decisions about whether we seek convergence or not.

The question (and the challenge) before us as scholars and practitioners is, How are we to use scarce resources effectively, maintain the integrity of our institutions and, most important, serve students and society well? How do the differences make a difference?

ELIZABETH M. HAWTHORNE is associate professor and director of academic affairs at Pennsylvania State University, Berks Campus, Reading.

INDEX

Ordering Information

New Directions for Community Colleges is a series of paperback books that provides expert assistance to help community colleges meet the challenges of their distinctive and expanding educational mission. Books in the series are published quarterly in Spring, Summer, Fall, and Winter and are available for purchase by subscription and individually.

Subscriptions for 1995 cost $49.00 for individuals (a savings of 35 percent over single-copy prices) and $72.00 for institutions, agencies, and libraries. Please do not send institutional checks for personal subscriptions. Standing orders are accepted. (For subscriptions outside of North America, add $7.00 for shipping via surface mail or $25.00 for air mail. Orders *must be prepaid* in U.S. dollars by check drawn on a U.S. bank or charged to VISA, MasterCard, or American Express.)

Single copies cost $19.00 plus shipping (see below) when payment accompanies order. California, New Jersey, New York, and Washington, D.C., residents please include appropriate sales tax. Canadian residents add GST and any local taxes. Billed orders will be charged shipping and handling. No billed shipments to post office boxes. (Orders from outside North America *must be prepaid* in U.S. dollars by check drawn on a U.S. bank or charged to VISA, MasterCard, or American Express.)

Shipping (Single Copies Only): one issue, add $3.50; two issues, add $4.50; three issues, add $5.50; four to five issues, add $6.50; six to seven issues, add $7.50; eight or more issues, add $8.50.

Discounts for quantity orders are available. Please write to the address below for information.

All orders must include either the name of an individual or an official purchase order number. Please submit your order as follows:
  Subscriptions: specify series and year subscription is to begin
  Single copies: include individual title code (such as CC82)

Mail all orders to:
  Jossey-Bass Publishers
  350 Sansome Street
  San Francisco, California 94104-1342

For subscription sales outside of the United States, contact any international subscription agency or Jossey-Bass directly.